The Art of SERIES

EDITED BY CHARLES BAXTER

The Art of series is a new line of books reinvigorating the practice of craft and criticism. Each book will be a brief, witty, and useful exploration of fiction, nonfiction, or poetry by a writer impassioned by a singular craft issue. *The Art of* volumes will provide a series of sustained examination of key, but sometimes neglected, aspects of creative writing by some of contemporary literature's finest practitioners.

THE ART OF

TIME IN MEMOIR

THEN, AGAIN

The Art of

TIME IN MEMOIR

THEN, AGAIN

Sven Birkerts

Graywolf Press

SAINT PAUL, MINNESOTA

Publication of this volume is made possible in part by a grant provided by
the Minnesota State Arts Board, through an appropriation by the Minnesota
State Legislature; a grant from the Wells Fargo Foundation Minnesota; and
a grant from the National Endowment for the Arts, which believes that a
great nation deserves great art. Significant support has also been provided
by the Bush Foundation; Target; the McKnight Foundation; and other gener-
ous contributions from foundations, corporations, and individuals. To these
organizations and individuals we offer our heartfelt thanks.

MINNESOTA STATE ARTS BOARD

NATIONAL ENDOWMENT FOR THE ARTS

TARGET.

Clara Ueland and Walt McCarthy are pleased to support the Graywolf Press
Art of series in honor of Brenda Ueland.

Published by Graywolf Press
2402 University Avenue, Suite 203
Saint Paul, Minnesota 55114
All rights reserved.

www.graywolfpress.org

Published in the United States of America

ISBN 978-1-55597-489-3

2 4 6 8 9 7 5 3 1
First Graywolf Printing, 2008

Library of Congress Control Number: 2007924774

Series cover design: Scott Sorenson

Cover art: Scott Sorenson

Life is not what one lived, but what one
remembers and how one remembers it
in order to recount it.

—Gabriel García Márquez

Contents

THE ART OF

TIME IN MEMOIR

THEN, AGAIN

The Time of Our Lives

If I had a dollar for every time some writer or student or chance acquaintance has confided to me their desire to write a memoir, I could buy myself a mossy castle in the west of Ireland and disappear once and for all into my private mythology. There's no getting around it: where we find the sense-making itch—the urge to capture and memorialize personal experience—there we find the scratching of pens. Or, far more likely, the chattering of keys. Memoir is, for better and often for worse, the genre of our times, and I have now read and worked with enough would-be memoirists to recognize the force of the need as well as some of the obstacles to its artistic realization. Again and again people say to me, "If I could just *tell* it," and I know exactly what they mean. But how hard it is to disabuse them of the idea that if they just started at the beginning and worked their way forward, all would be revealed. Wrong, wrong, wrong. There is in fact no faster way to smother the core meaning of a life, its elusive threads and connections, than with the heavy blanket of narrated event. Even the juiciest scandals and revelations topple before the drone of, "And then . . . and then . . ."

Memoir begins not with event but with the intuition of meaning—with the mysterious fact that life can sometimes step free from the chaos of contingency and become story. There is no telling when—or if—the transformation will come, and I am wary about universalizing. What reflections I offer are based on my own experience and necessarily provisional.

A curious thing happened to me personally and as a writer—I do make some slight distinction—when I entered my late forties, that time zone I reluctantly acknowledge as marking the onset of middle age. Quite suddenly, at least in retrospect, my relation to my own past changed. How can I describe it? It was as if that past, especially the events and feelings of my younger years, had taken a half step back, had overnight, following no effort on my part, arranged themselves into a perspective. No, "perspective" isn't quite right, for that suggests a fixed, even static arrangement. Rather, these materials had, without losing their animation or their savor, become available to me. They were there to be looked at and handled without as much of the usual emotional murkiness, with fewer complicating regrets, sadnesses, and so on.

More interesting still, those earlier years—from early childhood to the time of my late twenties—offered themselves to me as a mystery. I don't mean that there were crimes, literal or figurative, to get to the bottom of, only that behind the chronological accumulation of happenings, of this following that year after year, I discerned the possibility of hidden patterns, patterns that, if unearthed and understood, would somehow explain me—my life—to myself. These memories presented themselves discontinuously, as found bits of evidence, and I often felt, as they arrived, that they were trying to "tell" me something. I was possessed by the "stuff" of my own life, and on the strength of this I undertook—at first hesitantly, later with grim resolution—to write about those years of formation. A memoir had announced itself—though it was some time before I dared to apply that loaded term to what I was writing.

Why did this all happen when I was forty-eight and not when I was forty-five? What had changed in my psychic mix? I wish I knew. Or maybe I don't, for my inability to answer leaves a certain enigma intact at the heart of the enterprise. All I know is that there came a point in my life when the memories and feelings started coming in loud and clear. It was as if cause and effect had fallen into some new alignment. Things fit, but not so much side by side as associatively, in unforeseen orderings. I began to see that events and circumstances were not as contained as I had once thought, but were, rather, part of a complicated weave, their influence appearing and disappearing over long stretches. And with this came a changed understanding about time, that it was not, psychologically, a linear continuum—the whole business was much closer to four-dimensional chess, but even that is a simplification, for life contains four-dimensional chess and a good deal else.

As for trying to write about it, clearly 4-D chess would be an impossible model to try to follow. The best default seemed to be a work comprising at least two time lines—present and past. The now and the then (the many *thens*), for it is the juxtaposition of the two—in whatever configuration—that creates the quasi-spatial illusion most approximating the sensations of lived experience, of recollection merging into the ongoing business of living.

Now, then. Present, past. The sine qua non of memoir, with the past deepening and giving authority to the present, and the present (just by virtue of being invoked) creating the necessary depth of field for the persuasive idea of the past.

I won't dwell on the writing or its various revelations except as I need to, but I begin here because the undertaking allowed me to see how the search for patterns and connections is the real point—and glory—of the genre. And if I hurry to specify this aspiration, I do so to draw a sharp marking line between the kind of literary memoir I'm talking about and the sensation-driven (and all too often chronologically told) kind that has been getting so much airplay these last few years. Indeed, it seems that wherever I turn lately—allow the exaggeration for effect—I find another pundit or disgruntled editor bemoaning the much-publicized memoir "boom," more often than not declaring that it has, or will soon have, run its course. As if memoir were nothing more than a New Age excrescence, a latest fad, the apotheosis of a self-as-victim movement sponsored in equal parts by therapists, confession gurus, and scandalmongers eager to cash in on the bottomless societal appetite for self-exposing disclosure. Were you abused, neglected, discriminated against; did you turn in your pain to pills, drink, or satanic cults? Write a memoir!

But we cannot allow the many to wreck things for the few. The fact of rampant sensationalism must not be allowed to obscure the other fact, which is that recent decades have seen the flourishing of a sophisticated and quietly vital mode of literary expression. By which I don't mean to suggest that memoir itself is a recent coinage—what is St. Augustine's *Confessions* but a memoir?—only that in the last quarter century or so it has refurbished itself in an expressively contemporary way and that a tall stack of these works marks a genuine contribution to our literature. I'm thinking of, among others, Geoffrey Wolff's *The Duke of Deception,* Tobias Wolff's *This Boy's Life,* Frank Conroy's *Stop-Time,* Mary Karr's *The Liars' Club,* Lucy Grealy's *Autobiography of a Face,* Blake Morrison's *And When Did You Last See*

Your Father?, Michael Ondaatje's *Running in the Family,* Annie Dillard's *An American Childhood,* Eva Hoffman's *Lost in Translation,* Jo Ann Beard's *The Boys of My Youth,* Vivian Gornick's *Fierce Attachments,* Maureen Howard's *Facts of Life,* Rick Moody's *The Black Veil,* and Clark Blaise's *I Had a Father.*

What do these works have in common, other than their stylistic grace and honesty of disclosure? Apart from whatever painful or disturbing events they recount, their deeper ulterior purpose is to discover the nonsequential connections that allow those experiences to make larger sense; they are about circumstance becoming meaningful when seen from a certain remove. They all, to greater or lesser degree, use the vantage point of the present to gain access to what might be called the hidden narrative of the past. Each is in its own way an account of detection, a realized effort to assemble the puzzle of what happened in the light of subsequent realization. I think of the circular search patterns of Frank Conroy or Geoffrey Wolff, for example, how both writers use the narrow platform of an adult circumstance to launch their ambitious backward-flinging dives. In this, as in so many of the other strategies, we see the attempt at mastery, the push toward wisdom. Each account in some way proposes the idea that a life can be figured on the page as a destiny, a filling out of a meaningful design by circumstance, and that this happens once events and situations are understood not just in themselves but as stages *en route* to decisive self-recognition.

One of the first discoveries I made when I began to return in a reflective way to earlier parts of my life was that there was often very little connection between events that by rights ought to be capitalized—important trips, moves, friendships, deaths—and the experiences that had in fact left the most vivid deposit in memory. I remembered a passage that had always struck me in Marguerite Yourcenar's novel *Memoirs of Hadrian,* where she has this most philosophical of emperors confide: "I have a chronology of my own which is wholly unrelated to anything based on the founding of Rome, or on the era of the Olympiads. Fifteen years with the armies have lasted less long than a single morning at Athens." This seems to me the memoirist's guiding truth, and it is subversive, flying directly in the face of the pieties we live by.

I have come to recognize that memory is an irrational, even counterintuitive ecologist, obeying the most obscure private laws, and raising one of the central questions facing the memoirist. What are the terms of mattering; what was actually important? One of the distinguishing features of the dull and dutiful memoirs that crowd our display tables is that they measure all experience in terms of a standardized, or universalized, scale of values. But when I immersed myself in trying to write my life I began to think about the relation between the remembered detail and the "truth" of my own experience. I would catch myself repeating Ezra Pound's beautiful lines, "What thou lovest well remains, / the rest is dross." Coming face-to-face with the contradiction between what I felt should be important and what in fact *seemed* important, I could understand my project as the attempted working out of a problem. Mainly: What did my so-called real memories add up to? What were they telling me that was different from the authorized version I had of my life?

It's one thing to experience this recognition, quite another to put it into practice, to create a story, a readable and sensible narrative from what are often the unlikeliest preserved traces. To trust in the details is but the beginning. To work with them, using them as prompts and points of access, was, for me, to make a second discovery. This discovery, also hard to trust, was that the inward process of a life is in significant ways divorced from the outer. I mean, if remembered details are taken strictly as an index of importance, then it is possible that the whole scale of mattering is turned on its head. In my case, seemingly important periods— periods in which ostensibly big things happened—often disappeared like so many Atlantises, with nothing to be retrieved, while some outwardly trivial moments might offer themselves, luminous and precise down to their finest corrugations.

Before I can take the discussion any further I need to make clear the kind of memory and the kind of detail I'm talking about, and I'll do so by invoking the crucial Proustian distinction between voluntary and involuntary memory. This will take us right to the heart of the memoirist's enterprise, but before someone objects that Proust's *Remembrance of Things Past* is a novel, let me counter that of all novels it is probably the closest to memoir; that to write it Proust mined his life in a thousand ways and then applied to the whole the memoirist's sense of the true scales of mattering. The much-publicized workings of memory dictated the narrative focus, often pushing against the conventions of the novel, so that a minor character could receive much more attention than, say, the narrator Marcel's own father.

Proust, heavily influenced by the theories of philosopher Henri Bergson, exhaustively explored the literary dichotomy between voluntary and involuntary memory. In this scheme, voluntary memory is the mechanical retrieval function that gives us access to our assembled picture of the past and allows us to zero in on events and sensations as along a grid of recollection. Using voluntary memory, we can work our way back to the summer of 1975; we can establish that we were traveling in Europe, spending a week in London, staying in a hostel, visiting museums every day. We all know that patient focus on preserved materials will bring back troves of specific information—what we ate, what we paid—and we could write the account of our lives in this fashion, going over old credit-card receipts and applying the exteriorized procedure of biography to the stuff of personal experience. Indeed, Proust early on wrote many hundreds of pages in this more formulaic way before he experienced the breakthrough that led him to undertake the all-consuming discipline of *Remembrance.* It was only when he had his *madeleine* moment that he grasped the power of the other kind of memory, Bergson's involuntary memory, and understood that this alone was the gateway to the real past.

What happened—at least according to literary legend—was that the author, revisiting as an adult one of the sites of his childhood, stopped to take tea. When he automatically dunked the crusty little cake—the famous *petite madeleine*—into his tea, he found that his unpremeditated action released a stored association of overwhelming force. A single taste suddenly swamped him with the charged-up sensation of childhood, overpowering all factual ordering, and in the light of this visceral reaction his former approaches to his remembered experience came to seem irrelevant. The vital past, the living past, he realized, could not be systematically excavated; it lay distilled in the very details that had not been groomed into story, details that could only be fortuitously discovered. The *madeleine* experience initiated for him a whole chain of association, and from this he achieved the eventual restoration of an entire vanished world.

We cannot all be the Prousts of our own experience, but most memoirists will probably agree that the creation of their work depends a good deal on the workings of the involuntary memory. Not only do these recouped sensations throw open the door to the felt past, but the logic of their connection then helps determine the narrative strategy and infuses it with an underlying sense of *quest.* Recovered feeling forces the writer to start thinking about the possibilities of dramatic presentation.

Structure is seldom a given, however. I carried my own intuitions in stray form for a long time, trying to write my way into what I thought of as the "feeling world" of my childhood. But no matter how decisively I pledged to stay with the found detail and to hold fast to what I felt was the true—original—scale of mattering, the logic of the conventional narrative kept reasserting itself. How hard it was to just say *how it was,* the task Robert Lowell sets himself in his poem "Epilogue": "Yet why not say what happened? / Pray for the grace of accuracy / Vermeer gave to the sun's illumination /

stealing like the tide across a map / to his girl solid with yearning." But to get at this "grace of accuracy" meant going against the available frame, the convention that exerts such warping pressure on all of us.

I would remind myself of my real purpose, of the truth that I was after, the kinds of moments that perhaps held the key, by referring over and over to a single passage in Nabokov's *Speak, Memory.* It became my touchstone, my talisman, this short anecdotal reflection that seemed to sum up so much about the memoirist's enterprise. Here is Nabokov remembering an incident from 1904, when he was five and Russia and Japan were at war:

> But let me see. I had an even earlier association with that war. One afternoon at the beginning of the same year, in our St. Petersburg house, I was led down from the nursery into my father's study to say how-do-you-do to a friend of the family, General Kuropatkin. His thickset, uniform-encased body creaking slightly, he spread out to amuse me a handful of matches, on the divan where he was sitting, placed ten of them end to end to make a horizontal line, and said, "This is the sea in calm weather." Then he tipped up each pair so as to turn a straight line into a zigzag—and that was "a stormy sea." He scrambled the matches and was about to do, I hoped, a better trick when we were interrupted. His aide-de-camp was shown in and said

something to him. With a Russian, flustered grunt, Kuropatkin heavily rose from his seat, the loose matches jumping up on the divan as his weight left it. That day, he had been ordered to assume supreme command of the Russian Army in the Far East.

This incident had a special sequel fifteen years later, when at a certain point of my father's flight from Bolshevik-held St. Petersburg to southern Russia he was accosted while crossing a bridge, by an old man who looked like a gray-bearded peasant in his sheepskin coat. He asked my father for a light. The next moment each recognized the other. I hope old Kuropatkin, in his rustic disguise, managed to evade Soviet imprisonment, but that is not the point. What pleases me is the evolution of the match theme: those magic ones he had shown me had been trifled with and mislaid, and his armies had also vanished, and everything had fallen through, like my toy trains that, in the winter of 1904–05, in Wiesbaden, I tried to run over the frozen puddles in the grounds of the Hotel Oranien. The following of such thematic designs through one's life should be, I think, the true purpose of autobiography.

That last sentence brings together everything I've been talking about so far, and the passage can stand as an emblem for the subjective imperative that is at the root of this kind of writing. Think of it: in this grown

man's reconstruction of childhood a vast historical cata-
clysm is deliberately pushed off to the margins; hindsight understanding is almost completely resisted on
behalf of the matches on the divan, which is to say
on behalf of the locally vivid and completely solipsis-
tic perspective of a five-year-old boy (though of course
Nabokov relies on the corrective readerly response).
Monstrous as it may seem in a certain way, the presentation expresses the necessary monomania of childhood
as well as the memoirist's obsession with the themes—
the private meanings—of his life.

In two short paragraphs, then, Nabokov has condensed several of the most vital elements of memoir.
Not only is the matchstick anecdote itself an illustration of what could only be involuntary memory (it
seems too idiosyncratic and outwardly slight to have
been consciously preserved), a flash of time restored
with a fine sensuous precision ("With a Russian, flustered grunt, Kuropatkin heavily rose from his seat . . ."),
but it also brings together with an effortless economy
the two time perspectives that I contend are essential for the four-dimensional interrogation favored by
the genre. The moment of the past is positioned here
in both its original setting *and* in the relativistic continuum, as one factor among many in an equation still
being solved—as a chess piece (to be Nabokovian) in
play in a game yet undecided.

This manipulation of the double vantage point is the memoirist's single most powerful and adaptable technique, allowing for a complex temporal access. The writer deploys the time frame as needed—sparingly, as we will see with certain works—in order to achieve greater immersion in a particular period (generally the more distant past); or else, in some cases, with more regular alternation. The purpose decides the process. To stay in one vantage point is to foreground the fictional illusionism; to play the hindsight perspective against it is to undercut the illusionism by emphasizing the revision of perspectives and the incorporation of relativism. The latter counteracts the coma-inducing logic of, "If I just tell what happened . . ." and promotes the dramatizing of the process of realization, which is the real point.

The reader of memoirs can't fail to notice how many of them center upon the author's younger years and the period of coming-of-age. This should come as no surprise: where the main incentive for the writing is the exploration of discovered themes and connections, the staging of self-discovery, the early years are naturally the prime area of focus. What's more, as the most intense and fraught encounters on the way to separation and independence are often with family members—parents—a majority of contemporary memoirs turn significantly on struggles with the mother or the father. Often enough these break along lines of gender, with men writing of their fathers (Paul Auster, Geoffrey Wolff, Clark Blaise, Blake Morrison) and women their mothers (Mary Karr, Jamaica Kincaid, Vivian Gornick). Where the relationships have been traumatic—abusive—the presentation of painful events is often right at the core of the work.

In other memoirs the conflicts have been of a different order or scale, but the tactics of braiding and alternating time lines are still similar. The writers aim to give the reader a strong taste of the experience itself— what happened, what it was like—*and* to give account of resolution and realization, and for this both vantage points are available. In examining the styles of contemporary memoir, I will try to zero in on specific ways that different authors deploy both perspectives.

Chronicling the coming-of-age and family ordeals is of course not the sole purpose of the literary memoir. Writers like Nabokov or Virginia Woolf or Ondaatje make it clear in their works that researching the actions of memory can be purpose enough. They hardly need to apologize. In their pursuit of pure recollected sensation, these writers can be seen to be carrying out an inquiry into the dynamics of consciousness itself.

Nabokov, as so often, offers a perfect illustration. Indeed, he has put the archeology of memory at the dead center of his art. Here is part of an extended sensory description of his various tutors and governesses:

A large woman, a very stout woman, Mademoiselle
rolled into our existence in December 1905 when
I was six and my brother five. There she is. I see so
plainly her abundant dark hair, brushed up high and
covertly graying; the three wrinkles on her austere
forehead; her beetling brows; the steely eyes behind
the black-rimmed pince-nez; that vestigial mustache;
that blotchy complexion, which in moments of wrath
develops an additional flush in the region of the third,
and amplest, chin so regally spread over the frilled
mountain of her blouse. And now she sits down, or
rather she tackles the job of sitting down, the jelly
of her jowl quaking, her prodigious posterior, with
the three buttons on the side, lowering itself warily;
then, at the last second, she surrenders her bulk to
the wicker armchair, which, out of sheer fright, bursts
into a salvo of crackling.

The prose is stunning and argues for itself. But I can
also imagine a reader wondering just how important
to the scheme of things these fond detailings might be.
I have been that reader myself. I can remember how I
chafed at reading some of these sections of the memoir
when I was younger, growing more and more impatient
with what seemed to me Nabokov's endless fetishizing
of minutiae. I don't feel that way anymore. What happened? Is my change of mind somehow linked to that

more detached access to memory that I wrote about earlier? I can't be sure, but reading the passage now I delight in the vindication of the power of memory, the restoration through words of what has otherwise vanished from the world. It doesn't matter that I had no Mademoiselle, that there was no wicker armchair in our home. I had my own people, my own furniture. Employing a deep down substitution of terms, I engage. Just as essayist and memoirist André Aciman wrote of his experience of reading Proust: "The seductive power of a novel such as the *Search* lies in its personal invitation to each one of us to read Marcel's life as if we, and not Marcel, were its true subject."

Mention of Proust brings us back around to the question of genre. What special reach or access does memoir have that the novel does not? Given the enormous suppleness and variability of fiction, the answer can only have to do with the reality status of the subject matter. What gives the memoir its special title—and, I think, its growing rather than diminishing place in our literary culture—is the constraint of the actual. This constraint is the defining thing and requires some comment.

Some years ago, trying to explain the importance of biography in a postmodern world, I found myself making the argument that transformed social circumstances have in many ways made it harder and harder for people to "live a life" in the sense assumed by readers of biographies of outsized individuals. Who can deny it? The

rapid-fire digitizing of modern life has blurred and diminished our sense of the freestanding self. Increasingly
enslaved by our electronic extensions—our tools and
conveniences—we have a harder time living the kinds
of lives that can be given contour and written about. I'm
not suggesting—here, anyway—that we are less happy
or fulfilled, only that certain imaginative conceptions
of ourselves are harder to keep alive. For one thing, our
dealings with others are at every level more complexly
mediated; for another, these systems create an environment of easy and constant interaction, with the result
that our self-conception is necessarily more fragmented
and diluted.

To put it starkly: we are experiencing a crisis of representation in the arts, literature included. Artists and
writers are having an ever harder time giving memorable interpretative expression to the life of the present,
which is not their only task, of course, but certainly one
of the main ones. Literary novels that give voice to *how
it is* in our cultural moment are scarce, and for good
reason. So much of *how it is* is people living densely—
as complicatedly as ever before—but at one remove
from concrete settings, carrying on much of their work
and relationships by way of this grid of signals. Living
has become more ramified, more mental (if not more
reflective) and less concretely actual.

But we certainly haven't lost the need to feel ourselves as vitally and meaningfully alive. It's a favorite

theme of our therapy sessions, and this is not likely to change soon. New modes of access are wanted, new perspectives through which our late-modern lives can be understood. And this is one of the signal uses of the memoir. For whatever story the memoirist may tell, he or she is also at the same time modeling a way to re-flectively make sense of experience—using hindsight to follow the thread back into the labyrinth. Reading their work, we borrow their investigative energy and con-template similar ways of accessing our own lives.

There is a certain kinship between the memoirist's quest for the Jamesian "figure in the carpet" and the explorations and pattern searches of psychotherapy. But while the affinities are easily spotted, there is a significant difference. The work of therapy is private, and its goals of understanding and integration are not projected into the imagined public space of literature. They remain particular to the individual. The memoir-ist, by contrast, deploys many of the same energies of self-interrogation, but does so with the goal of discov-ering a narrative that will make sense, not just as expla-nation, but also as dramatization, to a would-be reader. She creates from the twining together of circumstance and reflection a story that needs no pre-understanding, offering up its own explanations and terms of interest.

For example, I may reflect in therapy on an un-happy period of my adolescence, testing memories and looking for insights that will help me understand why I did what I did *then.* To convert this into memoiristic material, however, I need to give the reader both the unprocessed feeling of the world as I saw it then *and* a reflective vantage point that incorporates or suggests that these events made a different kind of sense over time. This is the transformation that, if done well, absolves a memoiristic reflection from the charge of self-involved navel-gazing. What makes the difference is not only the fact of reflective self-awareness, but the conversion of private into public by way of a narrative compelling the interest and engagement of the reader. The act of storytelling—even if the story is an account of psychological self-realization—is by its very nature an attempt at universalizing the specific; it assumes there is a shared ground between the teller and the audience. Storytelling fails when the narrative cannot coax sympathetic resonance from the listener.

The contemporary memoir, then, assumes that the path of self-awareness, whether through the exploration of the process of coming-of-age, or through mastery of trauma, makes a universally relevant story that readers can apply as a supple screen to their very different experiences.

The sections that follow take up the memoirist's craft from several perspectives. The first contemplates the core impulse of the genre, which is to repossess the life of the past and to make it come alive, with special emphasis placed on raising the flame on what might be called the "Woolfian moment," and exposing in the process something of the essential nature of memory. Next I explore the question of self-making by looking at attempts by writers to give coherence as well as narrative momentum to the coming-of-age experience. I then examine various complex family relationships (and struggles), with special attention given to sons contending with fathers, and daughters with mothers. Finally, staying close to my originating premise, I question the memoirist's treatment of traumatic experience, trying to determine how realization and mastery are reflected in the structure of the telling. The author's manipulations of time are crucial, and while the sections cover as much of the subject terrain as they can, they also study from different angles how the play of time perspectives determines the dynamics of narration and allows the writer to bring the chaotic materials of experience into memorable shape.

Paradises Lost: The Lyrical Seekers

The memoirist writes, above all else, to redeem experience, to reawaken the past, and to find its pattern; better yet, he writes to discover behind bygone events a dramatic explanatory narrative. The deeper incentives vary. There are memoirists who were hurt into their art, suffering trauma or loss, and there are those who were pushed to language by the richness of their early lives. For some the event-based story of the past may be paramount—specific things happened that beg to be written about—while for others it may be the process of discovering that there *is* a story; and for still others the main incentive might be to connect with the elusive feelings and sensations of what happened so long ago.

This last group, which I think of as the lyrical seekers, offers us the clearest path to the fundamental ontological business of the genre of getting hold of vanished experience. I'll start by considering what three past-afflicted writers—Vladimir Nabokov, Virginia Woolf, and Annie Dillard—offer us in such distilled form: the sensuous apprehension of once-vivid circumstances and states of mind.

That joining of terms—"circumstances" and "states of mind"—is purposeful, for it seems to me that the two are always linked together in the memoirist's mind. The point of the recollection of thing, person, or event is in large part to reinhabit, to some degree, the former self, an essential step in trying to find the meaning of one's own experience.

Woolf addresses this matter straight off in her unfinished attempt at memoir, "A Sketch of the Past": "Here I come to one of the memoir writer's difficulties," she writes, "one of the reasons why, though I read so many, so many are failures. They leave out the person to whom things happened. The reason is that it is so difficult to describe any human being. So they say 'This is what happened'; but they do not say what the person was like to whom it happened. And the events mean very little unless we know first to whom they happened."

Woolf's point is crucial, and the would-be memoirist should heed it closely. The narrator, who is also the narrative subject, can't just be assumed. If the memoir is to be something more than a thin reportorial digest of events, if it is to *matter*, then the writer must create her identity on the page, making it as persuasive and compelling as that of any realized fictional protagonist. In other words, the memoirist's "I" must be an inhabited character, a voice that takes possession of its account. In memoirs where event and situation are paramount, the narrator achieves identity through decisions of self-presentation—what to reveal and from what vantage point—and tone. Is the writer bemused by the actions of the younger self, or moved to contemplate a former innocence? The reader responds to a whole gamut of clues. But what of writers more interested in states of awareness than specific circumstances? How do they catch hold of the fugitive self?

The three memoirists I focus on here are all in a sense philosophers of being who have taken themselves as subjects, as instances. They are all grounded in a metaphysical astonishment at the fact of existence, the signature expression of which is the lyrical mode—not for its own sake, not because a certain subtle or rich musicality of prose is pleasing, but because the re-creation of the kinds of sensations and accompanying states of consciousness they are after requires it. In the process, inescapably, they cannot but reflect almost continually, either directly or implicitly, on that which is at once the medium and object of the quest. Every memoirist is, with Proust, in search of lost time. It could hardly be otherwise with a genre that takes its very name from the instrument of recollection—memory.

If these memoirists are at some deep level philosophers of being, literally "lovers of the truth"—the truth of living—then I would argue that the specific details of their recollection, the trophies, are but the *means,* less important in themselves than for what they offer access to. I so often hear, from students especially, the "who cares?" complaint, as in, "Who cares that this writer can give us the texture of the couch he sat on as a child?" The point is well taken—unless there is some recognition that it is only by way of the texture of that couch, or carpet, that the writer (and, thus, reader) can grasp how the world presented itself back then, and therefore how it is that the past leaves its traces on the life. The detail is, in this sense, partly pretext. It functions for the memoirist as the piece of fruit does for the still-life painter—as an occasion for studying the nature of solidity, the play of light on objects, and the perceptual process.

If it's true that a core part of the memoirist's mission is a research into the nature of being, or consciousness—the two are profoundly linked—then it stands to reason that the writer will be drawn to an excavation of origins. And what greater prize could there be, in a sense, than the recovery of the earliest possible sensations, tokens of the encounter of self and world before the deformations of habit and expectation supervened? Here there is the possibility of ambush, of getting hold of the unschooled perception. So Nabokov will write at the beginning of *Speak, Memory:* "In probing my childhood (which is the next best to probing one's eternity) I see the awakening of consciousness as a series of spaced flashes, with the intervals between them gradually diminishing until bright blocks of perception are formed, affording memory a slippery hold."

Nabokov then isolates certain of these "flashes," which he identifies as coming when he was four years old, including a very important one having to do with the cognitive recognition of his parents *as* parents. "At that instant," he writes, "I became acutely aware that the twenty-seven-year-old being, in soft white and pink, holding my left hand, was my mother, and that the thirty-three-year-old being, in hard white and gold, holding my right hand, was my father." And then, just a few sentences on, in a perfect instance of narration braiding with hindsight reflection, he adds: "Indeed, from my present ridge of remote, isolated, almost uninhabited time, I see my diminutive self as celebrating, on that August day 1903, the birth of sentient life." The adjacency of perception and reflection makes clear that the memory is cherished not just for itself but also for the clues it offers toward solving for X—or, in this case, solving for N.

After this, Nabokov devotes some pages to the cataloging of specific retrievals, almost as if these detailed memories were fluttering specimens of the sort he would later pursue so obsessively. He re-creates for his reader the boyhood thrill of tunneling through a cave-like space behind a "big cretonne-covered divan, white with black trefoils" in the drawing room, and then, later, the impressions he preserves from looking out the window of the sleeping car of a train "and seeing with an inexplicable pang, a handful of fabulous lights that beckoned to me from a distant hillside, and then slipped into a pocket of black velvet." These details, he adds, "belong to the harmonious world of a perfect childhood and, as such, possess a naturally plastic form in one's memory, which can be set down with hardly any effort; it is only starting with the recollections of one's adolescence that Mnemosyne begins to get choosy and crabbed." What he doesn't say is that these same details, how they are registered and then arranged on the page, give the reader the sharpest awareness of the perceiving "I."

Nabokov rounds out this section with a statement that could serve as the banner inscription for the lyric memoirist: "Neither in environment nor in heredity can I find the exact instrument that fashioned me, the anonymous roller that pressed upon my life a certain intricate watermark whose unique design becomes visible when the lamp of art is made to shine through life's foolscap."

More, even, than Nabokov, that most time-besotted of memoirists, Virginia Woolf pushes upstream toward beginnings. In "A Sketch of the Past," she tries to get herself back to the very earliest of those "flashes" Nabokov invoked by locating sensation as it left its traces on the almost molten stuff of emerging consciousness. But she, too, is canny about working in the secondary, reflective voice.

Woolf begins her "memoir" with a calculated sort of dithering, giving us her location in time—April 1939—and letting us know that she is tired of her appointed task, writing the life of artist/critic Roger Fry, and that she plans to take just a few days off to write down her recollections of the past, her "memoirs." But then she finds herself right away weighing the various difficulties of the enterprise, finding the right approach. And in characteristic Woolfian fashion—much as she did in her celebrated essay "A Room of One's Own"—she figuratively hitches up her skirts and steps off into the field. "So," she writes, "without stopping to choose my way, in the sure and certain knowledge that it will find itself—or if not it will not matter—I begin: the first memory."

And here is the passage she offers:

This was of red and purple flowers on a black ground—my mother's dress; and she was sitting either on a train or in an omnibus, and I was on her lap. I therefore saw the flowers she was wearing very close; and can still see purple and red and blue, I think, against the black; they must have been anemones, I suppose. Perhaps we were going to St Ives; more probably, for from the light it must have been evening, we were coming back to London. But it is more convenient artistically to suppose that we were going to St Ives, for that will lead to my other memory, which also seems to be my first memory, and in fact it is the most important of all my memories. If life has a base that it stands upon, if it is a bowl that one fills and fills and fills—then my bowl without a doubt stands upon this memory. It is of lying half asleep, half awake, in bed in the nursery at St Ives. It is of hearing the waves breaking, one, two, one, two, and sending a splash of water over the beach; and then breaking, one, two, one, two, behind a yellow blind. It is of hearing the blind draw its little acorn across the floor as the wind blew the blind out. It is of lying and hearing this splash and seeing this light, and feeling, it is almost impossible that I should be here; of feeling the purest ecstasy I can conceive.

There are any number of things to point out here. First, linking to Nabokov's own foundation memory, is the mother connection, where physical nearness is coupled to a strong sensory awareness. Nabokov recalls his mother in "soft white and pink"; Woolf is fixated by the flowers on her mother's dress. In both cases the memory is narrated in such a way that we feel the child's sense of the parent's physical proximity and bulk. Neither memory is evaluated for its emotional suggestion.

In Woolf's case, though, there is a strategic staging—she admits to it herself—with mother and St. Ives already joined. How fitting, insofar as St. Ives was the setting of her most vivid childhood memories—the setting memorialized in *To the Lighthouse*—while her mother was the center of her emotional life, a recognition that is established in the pages of her memoir mainly through focus on the void left by her untimely death.

We note, too, Woolf's archly self-reflective aside—"it is more convenient artistically to suppose that we were going to St Ives, for that will lead to my other memory"—which reminds us, lest we ever forget, that a memoir is, whatever its pretenses to the contrary, a narrative conceit; it creates a structure that is the life shaped and disciplined to serve the pattern, the hindsight recognition that is deemed to be the larger, more important truth. Woolf is, in those phrases, asserting her artistic license, even as she is *en route* to netting all of those early perceptions in their concrete—their uncorrupted—particularity.

Finally, there is the remembered sensation itself, the base that, as Woolf affirms, the whole of her life stands upon. It is murky, rhythmic, auditory—mainly—conveying at one and the same time the barely differentiated immensity of ocean and the crisp distinctness of that "acorn" sounding against the floor. Of course we have to wonder in what sense this primary impression can be understood as a "base," a question that in Woolf's case is made more interesting when we consider the setting and atmosphere of her great novel about her family and her mother's death, *To the Lighthouse,* as well as the rhythmic and imagistic saturations of a work like *The Waves.*

As for her feeling the "purest ecstasy," the recognition, like Nabokov's sighting of those "fabulous lights" on the hillside, argues for the lyrical impulse being grounded in the amazement that is at the same time a short-circuiting of the senses by an overwhelming delight.

Annie Dillard's *An American Childhood* is likewise a lyrical memoir. Slightly more programmatic than either Nabokov or Woolf, Dillard sets out to capture her early years and her coming-of-age through a series of successive overlays. She has, in effect, tried to reinhabit each stage of her emerging awareness, laying hold of it from the inside by way of sensuous reconstruction, leaving the hindsight interpolations to a minimum, though as we will see, she does have some very important uses for this other voice.

Like Woolf, Dillard cites as one of her very earliest memories lying in her bed waiting for sleep. There is something about that watchful, tuned-up wakefulness— think of the opening pages of Proust, where Marcel lies in the dark willing his mother to come to him. Weren't these the hours, for many of us, when the sense of self first condensed into active awareness?

If Dillard is less prone to the reflective weave than Nabokov or Woolf, she still makes use of the distancing options it affords. For these scraps of early recovered memory are episodic, lacking narrative structure, and can't quite stand by themselves. And no doubt Dillard knows, instinctively as well as consciously, that the best effects are often achieved through an alternation of vantage points, where the highlighted sensation can stand out against a more general, or abstracted, background.

Dillard begins this section, then, with a set of broadly conceptual observations. "The interior life is often stupid," she writes, openly provoking all of us who would like to think the contrary. "Its egoism blinds it and deafens it; its imagination spins out ignorant tales, fascinated." And: "A mind risks real ignorance for the sometimes paltry prize of an imagination enriched. The trick of reason is to get the imagination to seize the actual world—if only from time to time." How this ambush might be arranged is not specified.

The author then gives us our basic narrative coordinates: "When I was five, growing up in Pittsburgh in 1950, I would not go to bed willingly because something came into my room. This was a private matter between me and it. If I spoke of it, it would kill me." This is not so much reflective hindsight as explanatory exposition on its way to scenic evocation, which she then begins with a depiction of the enviable sleep-state of her two-year-old sister, Amy, who shared her room: "All night long she slept smoothly in a series of pleasant and serene, if artificial-looking, positions, a faint smile on her closed lips, as if she were posing for an ad for sheets." Amy's blissful unconsciousness is artistically deployed as the backdrop to Dillard's own anxious wakefulness and her awareness of the other presence:

> I lay alone and was almost asleep when the damned thing entered the room by flattening itself against the open door and sliding in. It was a transparent, luminous oblong. I could see the door whiten at its touch; I could see the blue wall turn pale where it raced over it, and see the maple headboard of Amy's bed glow. It was a swift spirit; it was an awareness.

While it's true that Dillard is not as given to the sorts of leapfrogging time speculations that Nabokov and Woolf both delight in, she makes her adult writerly presence felt in another way. Far more than they, she models her remembered perceptions to give them shape. We feel, in this bit that recalls, of all things, Tinkerbell's arrival in the nursery in *Peter Pan,* the crafting of suspense; we feel the pressure of her desire for emphatic artistic effect giving form to what was very likely a less picturesque series of happenings.

The presence of the shaping hand is evident in a larger way as well, for Dillard has—we gradually realize—engineered the sequence carefully to achieve her desired end, which is to convey the double-take moment of recognition, the click that comes when she finally connects effect with cause and grasps that "it was a passing car whose windshield reflected the corner streetlight outside." The author here enacts in compressed form what the memoirist more commonly works out on the macroscale, namely, the collision of original perception and hindsight realization: the revision of the *then* by the *now.* Ever restless, Dillard does not stop; she takes the step to the next realization, which is that "the world did not have me in mind; it had no mind. It was a coincidental collection of things and people, of items, and I myself was one such item." And this, we understand, is what Dillard meant when she asserted that the inner life is "stupid."

But wait—it's not quite as simple as that. For such an understanding would basically establish existence itself as essentially contingent—accidental—and Dillard, a lyrical seeker, can't quite concede that. Her whole memoir is, in fact, an exploration of patterned consciousness, which in many ways *must* give lie to the idea of life as merely a "coincidental collection of things and people." And indeed, Dillard's next realization is strikingly characteristic of her writer's sensibility, at one and the same time caught up in the causal factuality of the world *and* open to the most venturesome flights of imagination.

When she is confronted with the empirical reality of the car and its lights, she finds her fantastical speculations abruptly stalled. Discovering herself at a kind of crossroads, she has a breakthrough: "I could be connected to the outer world by reason, if I chose, or I could yield to what amounted to a narrative fiction, to a tale of terror whispered to me by the blood in my ears, a show in light projected on the room's blue walls. As time passed, I learned to amuse myself in bed in the darkened room by entering the fiction deliberately and replacing it by reason deliberately." The traveler in Frost's yellow wood, she took both paths, and it made all the difference.

Dillard's strategic move of giving herself a double perspective—the factual and the imaginative—and making it actively conscious is defining for her memoir project as a whole, thus allowing her to follow her structural program of repossessing one stage after another of her own psychological growth, her coming-of-age, doing so in a way faithful to experience; it also gives her the license of imagination. She can, to a degree, impose story upon sequence, endowing it with pattern.

She does this in a number of ways in *An American Childhood.* She begins the book with a kind of Huck Finn narrative about her restless father who, when she was still a young girl, left the family for a time to sail the American riverways in his boat. He ultimately returns to resume parental duties, but not before infecting Dillard—and the memoir—with intimations of freedom and of chasing private dreams.

That is one kind of imaginative injection—the decision to enfold her fairly homebound childhood in a tantalizing family legend. On a very different level we find Dillard crafting what might be called an "emblem moment," a psychologically rich scene of recognition that she eventually returns to, achieving in this way a powerful effect of experience at last gathering into shape. This lends her account a much-needed sense of closure, reassuring the reader that the long chronicling of her girlhood wasn't just a recording of events and stages, but a going *toward,* a deliberate mapping of a self evolving from simpler to more complex levels of awareness.

Early in the book, in a lyric section in which she tries to capture the sensation of wakening to the world, to a larger sense of self—the end of the dream of childhood—Dillard makes use of a generalized bathtub scene, probing the memory to get at the slippery sense of double consciousness. Looking to capture the singular experience of merging selves, she writes:

> I never woke, at first, without recalling, chilled, all those other waking times, those similar stark views

from similarly lighted precipices: dizzying precipices
from which the distant, glittering world revealed
itself as a brooding and separated scene—and so
let slip a queer implication, that I myself was both
observer and observable, and so a possible object of
my own humming awareness. Whenever I stepped
into the porcelain bathtub, the bath's hot water sent
a shock traveling up my bones. The skin on my arms
pricked up, and the hair rose on the back of my skull.
I saw my own firm foot press the tub, and the pale
shadows waver over it, as if I were looking down from
the sky and remembering this scene forever. The
skin on my face tightened, as it had done whenever
I stepped into the tub, and remembering it all drew
a swinging line, loops connecting the dots, all the way
back. You again.

This is a girl's Proustian moment, an association
unexpectedly gathering the past to itself and bringing
with it a profound sensation of completion. Coming at
the end of Dillard's Prologue, it frees her to wind back
to earliest memories, laying down scene after scene, each
like a frame of a film that, if set into motion, might speed
up to depict at once the inward and outward growth of
a person.

Significantly, Dillard returns to the bath image at the
very end of the memoir, and through repetition gets us

to feel how much has happened, how many years have passed since she was that little girl. Indeed, it telegraphs her double theme—which is both the inevitability of change and the affirming persistence of self through change:

> Your very cells have been replaced, and so have most of your feelings—except for two, two that connect back as far as you can remember. One is the chilling sensation of lowering one foot into a hot bath. The other, which can and does occur at any time, never fails to occur when you lower one foot into a hot bath, and when you feel the chill spread inside your shoulders, shoot down your arms and rise to your lips, and when you remember having felt this sensation from always, from when your mother lifted you down toward the bath and you curled up your legs: it is the dizzying overreal sensation of noticing that you are here. You feel life wipe your face like a big brush.

We're back to that primal amazement at being that is the core incentive of the lyrical memoirist. Dillard, coming to this moment, doesn't pretend to have solved a problem. It's more that she has found continuity among change, an underlying self there among all the versions of self that growing up requires. With a single sensuous image she has created a chain of connection going all the way back, right into her mother's arms.

Virginia Woolf's version of essential selfhood, while likewise drawing together past and present, makes use of a somewhat different conception. Woolf creates for herself a primary opposition between the exceptional and the ordinary, between "being" and "non-being," and proposes that a great deal of our experience comprises the "cotton wool" of nonbeing. Whole days in childhood, as in adulthood, are lost because nothing makes them stand out; they are swallowed by routine.

But then there are the important moments, the ones that matter. They deliver some shock of awareness, though they're not themselves outwardly remarkable. These moments become the stuff of our memories and the core materials of our sense of self.

In "A Sketch of the Past," Woolf devotes considerable space to recounting and probing the memories that she has hoarded up for herself. Some, like Dillard's memory of the ectoplasmic shape on the wall suddenly finding explanation, are moments of realization. "I was looking at the flower bed by the front door," she writes, coming right to an epiphany. "'That is the whole,' I said. I was looking at a plant with a spread of leaves; and it seemed suddenly plain that the flower itself was a part of the earth."

Other memories are less obviously instructional. They just *are*, like the memory of Justine Nonon: "She was immensely old. Little hairs sprouted on her long bony chin. She was a hunchback; and walked like a spider, feeling her way with her long dry fingers from one chair to another." It's easy enough to imagine why this impression stuck with young Virginia.

Woolf feels her own way forward in her "Sketch," first coming up with her theory of salient moments and the cotton-wool batting of the ordinary, then going on for some pages setting out one remembered scene after another, mortaring them together with her own unique reflective asides. But before long she is pushing toward a new notion, one that argues for the need to plait together past and present:

> 2nd May . . . I write the date, because I think I have discovered a possible form for these notes. That is, to make them include the present—at least enough of the present to serve as platform to stand upon. It would be interesting to make the two people, I now, I then, come out in contrast. And further, this past is much affected by the present moment. What I write today I should not write in a year's time.

Woolf's plan is implemented only sketchily—we never do get a clear double portrait. Instead, she follows the gusts of her recollections where they blow, trusting that the luminous moments somehow compose a meaningful trail. Episodically, she will intrude the present, as here, where another dated entry marks the collision of the now and then:

> 19th July 1939. I was forced to break off again, and rather suspect that these breaks will be the end of this memoir.
>
> I was thinking about Stella as we crossed the Channel a month ago. I have not given her a thought since. The past only comes back when the present runs so smoothly that it is like the sliding surface of a deep river. Then one sees through the surface to the depths. In those moments I find one of my greatest satisfactions, not that I am thinking of the past; but it is then that I am living most fully in the present. For the present when backed by the past is a thousand times deeper than the present when it presses so close that you can feel nothing else, when the film on the camera reaches only the eye.

Perceptions like this are what make us turn to Woolf's memoir. If she hasn't discovered an artistic shape that will completely express the tension between present and past, she is nonetheless subjecting the mystery to a constant pressure of inquiry. My guess is that the work has the status of a draft, that it represents a preliminary staking out of territory, and that if Woolf had labored over it the way she labored over her novels, she would have eventually produced a more consistently resonant work. Passage after passage contain clues, hints of how her mind was working on the problem of self in time, enough to point to a larger, more synthetic work.

Reflecting on what it is that makes certain incidents and perceptions from the past stand out, Woolf theorizes that in some way they have provided a shock to the system. The passage can stand as a kind of manifesto or artist's statement, one especially applicable to the memoirist's enterprise: "I only know that many of these exceptional moments brought with them a peculiar horror and a physical collapse; they seemed dominant; myself passive. This suggests that as one gets older one has greater power through reason to provide an explanation; and that this explanation blunts the sledge-hammer force of the blow." The insight goes perfectly with Dillard's bedroom memory, the vividness of the imagining as it is then caged inside the bars of explanation.

Woolf continues:

I think this is true, because though I still have the peculiarity that I receive these sudden shocks, they are now always welcome; after the first surprise I always feel instantly that they are particularly valuable. And so I go on to suppose that the shock-receiving capacity is what makes me a writer. I hazard the explanation that a shock is at once in my case followed by the desire to explain it. I feel that I have had a blow; but it is not, as I thought as a child, simply a blow from an enemy hidden behind the cotton wool of daily life; it is or will become a revelation of some order; it is a token of some real thing behind appearances; and I make it real by putting it into words. . . . Perhaps this is the strongest pleasure known to me. It is the rapture I get when in writing I seem to be discovering what belongs to what . . . From this I reach what I might call a philosophy . . . that behind the cotton wool is hidden a pattern; that we—I mean all human beings—are connected with this; that the whole world is a work of art.

This demon of an idea, that there may be a pattern hidden behind the contingent-seeming procession of circumstance, is powerful in Woolf, and nearly over-powering in Nabokov. From his early presentation of the thought that his life is like a paper surface on which an "anonymous roller" has embossed a "certain intri-cate watermark," an image then revealed by the "lamp of art," to his embellishment of the "match theme" linking his associations with old General Kuropatkin, he is consistently finding analogies and metaphors that will make his intuition vivid.

One of the most memorable is his image midway through *Speak, Memory* of the magic carpet. Nabokov leads up to what is finally an announcement of his artistic credo (expressed as a kind of anticredo) with an extended description of his ecstatic pursuit of butterflies near his boyhood home. The prose is Nabokov at his most sensory. "Unmindful of the mosquitoes that furred my forearms," he writes, "I stooped with a grunt of delight to snuff out the life of some silver-studded lepidopteron throbbing in the folds of my net. Through the smells of the bog, I caught the subtle perfume of butterfly wings on my fingers." He pushes on for a few more sentences before ascending still higher:

I confess I do not believe in time. I like to fold my magic carpet, after use, in such a way as to superimpose one part of the pattern upon another. Let visitors trip. And the highest enjoyment of timelessness—in a landscape selected at random—is when I stand among rare butterflies and their food plants. This is ecstasy, and behind the ecstasy is something else, which is hard to explain. It is like a momentary vacuum into which rushes all that I love. A sense of oneness with sun and stone. A thrill of gratitude to whom it may concern—to the contrapuntal genius of human fate or to tender ghosts humoring a lucky mortal.

Like Woolf with her connecting of shocks to patterned meanings, Nabokov confesses to an almost visionary fulfillment, as if the artistic recognition of one shape matching to another across time (the folded carpet) springs him loose from the illusion of time-as-succession, allowing all that he loves to mingle together.

It's his obsession, this joining of things scattered in time, and just as Dillard concludes her memoir with the image of related moments summoned together by a single gesture—putting the foot in the hot bathwater—so Nabokov wraps up with the memory of watching his own son at the seashore bringing him and his wife his trophies, various shells, pebbles, and shards of pottery. Linking not just the moments of his own experience but also those of vanished generations, he writes:

> I do not doubt that among those slightly convex chips of majolica ware found by our child there was one whose border of scrollwork fitted exactly, and continued, the pattern of a fragment I had found in 1903 on the same shore, and that the two tallied with a third my mother had found on that Mentone beach in 1882, and with a fourth piece of the same pottery that had

been found by *her* mother a hundred years ago—and so on, until this assortment of parts, if all had been preserved, might have been put together to make the complete, the absolutely complete, bowl, broken by some Italian child, God knows where and when, and now mended by *these* rivets of bronze.

The lyrical memoirists are all, in their own fashion, ecstatic dreamers. Highly susceptible to loss and change, they use their work as a tool of restoration, searching out recurrences and patterns, but also then allowing for the idea that pattern hints at a larger order, possibly an intention to underlying experience. The memoirist researches this, using the self as subject, assembling the shards, riveting his impressions together word by word.

Coming-of-Age

Although memoirs cover a vast range of styles and subject matters—everything from J. R. Ackerley's *My Dog Tulip*, a life refracted through the prism of a canine adoration, to W. S. Merwin's almost stationary scene magnifications in *Unframed Originals*—far and away the most common are the authors' accounts of their coming-of-age. There are good and obvious reasons for this, but to approach these I would like to make what I think is a clarifying distinction between "memoir" and "autobiography." The two terms, often used as if they were synonymous, are actually labels for very different approaches to the project of writing about one's life and coming-of-age.

Part of the confusion arises from the fact that memoir is, in its fundamental nature, autobiographical, at least in the popular sense of being about the self. Autobiography, however, is not in any essential way memoiristic, and if we put a bit of pressure on the root meanings of the words the difference will come clear.

"Autobiography" divides as neatly as Gaul into its three source elements: "Auto," or *self;* "bio," or *life;* "graphy," or *line.* The line of one's own life. No mystery there: the autobiographer undertakes to set down the line of his or her life. Implicit is the sense of the comprehensive, the inclusive, as well as the promise of at least an attempted objectivity. Although some self-interpretation is inevitable, as are certain adjustments of focus and lighting, there is still the expectation that the view is in some sense exteriorized—the line, or development, of the life seen as if from without. A deliberately stylized instance of this is Henry Adams's decision in *The Education of Henry Adams* to recount the developments of his life in the third person. "This problem of education," writes Adams, "started in 1838, went on for three years, while the baby grew, like other babies, unconsciously, as a vegetable, the outside world working as it never had worked before, to get his new universe ready for him."

Since the purpose of these works is to track events over time, most autobiographies—and there haven't been many examples in the last years—are written by their authors in later life, when the line is longer and there is more sequence to document. Unless the writer manages to put the period to the last sentence with his final breath, an autobiography is necessarily unfinished, and theoretically liable to considerable revision. The narrated life of a seemingly honorable public figure, brought to happy conclusion in his seventieth year, will change status abruptly when, in his seventy-second year, he is exposed as the subject of a long-concealed scandal.

Memoirs, by contrast, are neither open ended nor provisional. For as the root of the word attests, they present not the line of the life but the life remembered. They are pledged not to an ostensibly detached accounting of events but to presentation of life as it is narratively reconstituted by memory. The memoirist is generally not after the sequenced account of his life so much as the story or stories that have given that life its internal shape. These are necessarily filtered by the memory and recounted in ways that reflect understanding and interpretation—in some cases to the point where the process of coming to understanding *is* the main part of the story. And because we come to our insights more by way of thematic association than chronology, using hindsight to pick the lock of the *then,* the structure of the work seldom follows the A-B-C of logical sequence.

Serving theme rather than event, memoir is far more selective than autobiography. Seasons, years, entire subplot developments are often elided. In fact, the narrative is often confined to the presentation of an interval, a phase, of the author's life—or, commonly, of the author's coming-of-age. A work can narrow its telling to a single thematic concern, as in Kathryn Harrison's *The Kiss,* which zeroes in on the brutal psychological fallout from an incestuous relationship; but it can also widen to encompass several generations in pursuit of the sources of family legend in a work like

Michael Ondaatje's *Running in the Family.* The scope is variable and is determined by the object of the author's private search. The point of the work, by and large, is to discover through memory the linkages that give resonance to what would otherwise be the chaos of the life.

This brings us, in somewhat roundabout fashion, to the question of why there are so many contemporary coming-of-age memoirs—enough of them to form the largest of the genre's subgenres. I'm thinking of works like Tobias Wolff's *This Boy's Life,* Geoffrey Wolff's *The Duke of Deception,* Paul Auster's *The Invention of Solitude,* Mary Karr's *The Liars' Club,* Maureen Howard's *Facts of Life,* Frank Conroy's *Stop-Time,* Clark Blaise's *I Had a Father,* Jo Ann Beard's *The Boys of My Youth,* Jamaica Kincaid's *Annie John,* Blake Morrison's *And When Did You Last See Your Father?,* and the list goes on and on, testifying to the vitality of the impulse.

To venture a broad generalization: our coming-of-age, however we define it—and I certainly include the childhood years as part of the mix—is the most dramatically fraught period of our lives. Relationships and myriad circumstances impinge directly on the formation of identity, and from the vantage point of retrospect (the memoirist's natural perch), they tell a story: this is how I came to be who I now am. Here were the influences, the choices; these were the paths taken, these the ones refused. Although the stakes and levels of intensity will differ from person to person, everyone has a story.

My own memoir was very much a coming-of-age saga, and the writing process turned out to be a kind of detached psychotherapy (though, alas, it did not eliminate either the need for or interest in the more expensive kind). I remember that I had felt for some years the buildup of a specific sort of pressure: the desire to break from writing literary essays and to reflect instead on my own life. I can't say what caused this, but it felt deep and necessary; it didn't feel like an opportunistic bid for fresh subject matter. Only in my late forties, though, did I begin to write memoiristic reflections, thinking of them for a long time as a potential series of personal essays. But the plan slowly changed. The more I found myself dwelling on my younger years, and on my family background—on stories that my parents had passed along about their lives and the lives of *their* parents—the more I felt that I was working on something bigger, more consecutive. I was trying to solve a kind of equation. I was increasingly interested in figuring out how the combination of personalities, circumstances, and influences *back then* had helped determine where I ended up. It seemed possible. No, more than that, it seemed *essential.* At the same time, as if to confirm that this was what I had to be doing, my memory life, long dormant, became active. Day after day I would have Proustian surprises, images from my past surfacing in my thoughts, often tagged with the sense that "this is important."

Gradually the impulse grew those sections into a full-scale project and the individually conceived personal essays linked up into something more complex—a memoir. But the reflective essayistic approach carried over. I still wanted there to be a blend of perspectives throughout, with the unfolding episodes accessible to hindsight contemplation—a kind of looking through time at myself *in* time.

But I hadn't figured out my genre yet. For many months, I know, I was still thinking in semiautobiographical terms. I envisioned my chapters marching me year by year right into the present, bringing me up-to-date, exploring the phases and vicissitudes of marriage, parenting, and the writing life itself. I had to go through many botched pages and much frustration before I understood that there was a problem with my conception: I was trying to blend two kinds of narration that did not fit easily together.

What I finally realized was this: the first three decades of my life—until I was in my late twenties—were all about formation, struggle, and search. Back then I didn't know if I could find a lasting relationship; I didn't know if I could make my way as a writer. There was a great deal of fumbling on both fronts. But as things fell out (owing to fate, or chance—this was, and still *is*, under investigation), when I was twenty-seven, in what retrospectively looks like a very compressed period of time, I met the woman I would some years later marry, *and* I wrote and published a long essay, a project that finally showed me what kind of writing I wanted to do. Although I didn't know it then, or think of it in this way, my coming-of-age was in some deep-down sense complete.

I discovered all this gradually and painfully as I tried to write in some episodic/reflective way about developments in my thirties and beyond. Bear down how I would, I could feel my urgency and focus leaking away. It didn't matter how I tried to rev up event sequences and heighten moments of conflict, the fact was that the underlying drama had gone out of my narrative. While the events of my earlier life were all filled with a pressing sense of the unknown—what would I end up *doing* with my life?—there did finally come a point when I knew, as much as anyone ever does. Clichéd as it may sound, I had gone through my appointed rites of passage. And once I understood this, and understood how this related to my memoir-in-progress, I was able to see the shape of the work, that it effectively ended with me at twenty-seven, in a stable relationship, beginning my writing life.

The memoirist, more than the novelist or poet, finds himself accused of navel-gazing, of unseemly self-involvement—the old "who cares if your dog Rex was hit by a car when you were ten?" challenge—and rebuttal is not that easy. For at some level it's true—necessarily—that the self-chronicler, possibly more than most mere mortals, *is* fascinated by the minutiae of his own experience. But thankfully the matter is more complex than that. The fact is, as I asserted earlier, citing Nabokov, that the specificity of remembered details exposes the universal dynamics of memory. Hearing the crackling of Mademoiselle lowering herself into the wicker chair brings our own sense memories closer. Indeed, done well, any writer's presentation of her coming-of-age puts us into active contemplation of the passages we endured in our own younger years. Specificity allows the scenes to come alive, and as they come alive they inevitably activate certain archetypes, whether these have to do with rebellion, sexual longing, friendship, betrayal, leave-taking . . .

The writing of the coming-of-age memoir proposes its own structural problems. I suggested how more lyrical writers like Nabokov and Woolf sought to impart some narrative dynamism to their sequences of recovered memories—most of them isolated moments of awareness rather than stories—how they reflectively dramatized the search for concealed patterns; and how Annie Dillard deployed recollected details to lend contour to successive stages of awareness, using that growth sequence as the structure of the work.

The coming-of-age memoirists are in a different situation. Unlike the lyricists, who find their main tension and interest in the dynamic shifts of consciousness itself, these writers have identified a less interior narrative progression; they have a story, as well as some culminating recognition toward which events will move. Their task is to find an expressive form, and a way to implement—or suggest—the transformations that come *en route.* Their use of reflection, of the hindsight perspective, is necessarily different from what we find in the work of their more lyrical counterparts.

Pledged like all memoirists to Mnemosyne, the muse of memory, those who recount the legend of self-formation must reckon with the fact that their deeper story, too, is discontinuous, that the events they would recount only disclose their significance over time, once it comes clear which aspects were meaningful in the light of eventual outcomes. In one way or another, then, the narrative must convey the movement of awareness. This can either be done directly, through staged epiphanies, or else suggestively, through various kinds of juxtapositions; both, as we'll see, allow for some manipulation of the reflective voice.

The presentation of epiphanic recognitions is problematic. I realized this in my own attempts at depicting my years of growing up. For realizations about life—one's own life and life in general—very often happen gradually, or else they come long after the fact, as delayed reactions. Hardly ever does some event lead one to a simple "aha!" from which new initiatives then naturally arise. That, at least, is the close-focus reality. But we should also note the fact that when one looks back as a memoirist—a god presiding over his own experience—there is a natural impulse to heighten and compress—to create what looks like a plot where in fact there was only ever the chaos of dailiness. And yet for some of us, these accounts of growth and change make a story and insist on being told that way.

I have said this already, but it bears repeated stressing: writers just starting to work with memoir often have a real difficulty with this crucial distinction between event sequence and story. The impulse to tell sequentially works with gravity-like force, generating structures that sag from the tedium of "and then . . . and then . . ." recounting and produce dense thickets of ostensibly relevant information. The writer gets the dread feeling that everything belongs, that important moments only make sense when all the facts have been presented. Every first-time memoirist comes up against it—the demon of infinite regress. To get this, you have to know that. That Grandma Kate never loved Grandpa Jacob is essential information—without it we would never know why Loretta, the mother, was so depressed. To get the narrator born can become an epic accomplishment—as Laurence Sterne's *Tristram Shandy* attests.

Not only is the sequential approach a chore for the writer, but it's often a deadly bore for the reader. The point is *story*, not chronology, and in memoir the story all but requires the dramatic ordering that hindsight affords. The question is not what happened when, but what, for the writer, was the path of realization, and it is the highlighting of this that overturns the tyranny of the linear and allows the subtle, or obvious, implementation of the after-the-fact perspective.

Keeping this in mind, I would then ask: How does the coming-of-age memoirist orchestrate the long and muddled business of self-discovery? Of course there are different strategies, and these are to some extent determined by the nature of the experience. Survivors of arduous, traumatic—or to use the popular adjective, "dysfunctional"—situations often have more scenic resources to work with: crises structure presentation more overtly. They have a natural dynamic of escalation, eruption, and consequence, and—one hopes—recovery. Similarly, those who grew up locked in a powerful psychological struggle with a parent—as we'll also see— have their own inevitable tensions and escalations and culminations to put across. But what about the writer who wants to give account of the whole panorama, to present in nondramatic fashion a full array of characters, circumstances, and transitional breakthroughs?

While there are any number of memoirs that fall into this general category, I'll point to three that find different narrative solutions to the problem of organizing the essentially inchoate materials of life into memoir form, and, also, to the linked problem of how to implement the secondary perspective without which there is no true memoir.

Frank Conroy's *Stop-Time*, first published in 1967, might be considered the paradigmatic coming-of-age memoir. It has all the elements of the genre: the sensitive, alienated narrator; the family turmoil; the first sexual awakenings; conflict with authorities; and, finally, departure and return. This last—Conroy's account of traveling to Europe to study and then coming back to America— would be almost enough by itself to create the narrative closure so important to the genre, especially this rites-of-passage category, where presenting the ending of one epoch and the beginning of another is very nearly a given.

But Conroy came up with another strategy as well. By adding four paragraphs of Prologue and then appending a few more paragraphs at the end as Epilogue, he intrudes a new time frame and radically changes how the reader will understand his story. While these are not his only uses of a secondary time frame—he incorporates short hindsight reflections and asides throughout—they are dramatically decisive in a way that the others are not.

The Prologue opens in the past tense: "When we were in England I worked well. Four or five hundred words every afternoon. We lived in a small house in the countryside about twenty miles south of London." But Conroy quickly undermines this impression of productive calm: "I would go to London once or twice a week in a wild, escalating passion of frustration, blinded by some mysterious mixture of guilt, moroseness, and desire." He headed into the city to get drunk, and then he would drive home in the early morning hours in his Jaguar, flashing through the empty streets of the city, and then opening up to suicidal speeds when he reached the countryside. Once, he claims, he even hit a hundred and fifteen on "the narrow, moonlit English road." He would do anything, he writes, "mounting the sidewalks, running red lights—anything at all to keep the speed, to maintain the speed and streak through the dark world." End of Prologue.

The reader hardly knows what to make of this, trusts that more will be revealed, even as it is clear on the next page that Conroy is going back to origins, beginning now with the fact that his father stopped living with his family when the author was three or four. Our likely first thought is that this account—the one that Conroy was presumably working on in England—will present an accrual of damages, eventually offering a convincing psychological explanation for this "mysterious mixture of guilt, moroseness, and desire" he feels. And to some extent this is just what happens.

But the business isn't quite so simple. For one thing, as the chapters follow each other, we start to forget the troubled velocity of the Prologue and find ourselves drawn instead into an absorbing set of developments, vivid scenic accounts that animate Conroy's boyhood, early relationships, and so on. Not until we are well into *Stop-Time* does the brooding, alienated mood begin to take over.

I don't have the space I would need to unpack the episodes of the memoir as they deserve, tracing out how subtle hindsight observations control the presentation, allowing us to remain essentially immersed in the episodic narrative, but also reminding us that there is a *later,* an authorial present in which these events are reexperienced and reevaluated. One instance will have to stand in for many.

Early in *Stop-Time,* Conroy is recalling an incident of sadistic violence from his time at a boarding school in Pennsylvania. The scenario is one familiar from movies: a group of boys gathers to inflict violence on a misfit, in this case a boy named Ligget. Conroy joins in with the others, throws the hardest punch he can, and at the end of the hazing session Ligget's jaw is broken in four places. But for various reasons the offense is tolerated; the school authorities finally mete out no punishment. Conroy himself engages in no direct self-accounting.

But then at chapter's end—and a switch this abrupt is uncharacteristic—he describes a scene from a much later time where he is lying in bed next to his wife, unable to sleep, and in what feels suddenly like a Nabokovian, or Woolfian, moment, he observes: "My faith in the firmness of time slips away gradually. I begin to believe that chronological time is an illusion and that some other principle organizes experience." And, a few sentences on: "I get so uncomfortable floating around like this that I almost gratefully accept the delusion that I've lived another life, remote from me now, and completely forgotten about it. Somewhere in the nooks and crannies of memory there are clues." Put in proximity to the hazing memory, his metaphysical speculation here clearly serves Conroy's psychological need to distance himself from, if not deny altogether, the unpleasant aspect of his younger self.

But this is an unusual amount of exposure for Conroy to offer. Most of his intrusions have the effect of sidelong observations, even if their ultimate import is more consequential. Remembering, for instance, an incident where Donald, a man staying with Conroy's family, plays a humiliating practical joke on his step-father, Jean, he sets the moment up thus: "For a fraction of a second there was silence, and in that small full instant I changed, I aged. I understood hate for the first time." The recognition is supplied by the adult looking back, but it has been worked into the scene in such a way that we are not pulled from the spell of the moment, as we were, earlier, when Conroy gave us a picture of himself lying beside his sleeping wife.

For the most part, Conroy keeps us inside the fabricated illusion of the *then*, the recollection. So much so, in fact, that we have most likely put the scene of the speeding Jaguar from our thoughts. We are immersed in the lonely vicissitudes of his isolated boyhood, his high school years, his trip to Europe, and when he sails home right near memoir's end, we respond to the structural cues. Return equals completion—the coming-of-age cycle, with all its angst and yearning, is done with. We assume that whatever life brings next will be different.

What a shock, then, to hit the brief Epilogue. With the turn of a page we are back in England, back in the careening Jaguar, and Conroy, driving, is evidently very drunk and beyond all caring. The momentum builds until he finally loses control: "I looked out the open window toward the fountain. It was coming directly at me, coming very fast as the car skidded broadside across the square. . . . I was going to die. As the fountain grew larger I felt myself relax."

Conroy doesn't die, of course, but he has given us a flash portrait of his soul, and in this moment we are forced to revise our earlier determinations. If we had thought that the young man's return to America had put the lid on the confusions and losses of his younger years, we were wrong. He is clearly a man in pain. And if we had thought that the writing of his life in memoir form was ultimately a gesture of redemption, we were wrong about that, too. No, defiant of a more aestheticized view, a view such as Nabokov certainly held, Conroy draws the line between the life and the art, even as his act of writing represents a constant effort to merge the two.

I have in front of me a paperback copy of Jo Ann Beard's *The Boys of My Youth,* and what a baffling item it is. The shelving tag on the top of the back cover identifies it as: MEMOIR/ESSAYS, while directly underneath, Barbara Fisher's blurb, taken from her review in the *Boston Globe,* raves: "This is what a first collection of stories should be." The publisher's description just below that calls the book a "widely praised collection of autobiographical essays."

If the confusion indicates anything, I think, it's less a doubt about the veracity of the separate pieces and more an uncertainty about whether certain kinds of "artistic" arrangements of autobiographical materials must not automatically be regarded as "fictions." Is this

what Barbara Fisher had in mind in referring to the
book as a collection of stories? How much structural
choreography *is* a writer permitted with the stuff of her
own experience? Does a certain level of self-conscious
"art" remove fact to the category of the invented?

There is no rule book to refer to. The only criterion
I can imagine invoking here is that of final effect. Does
the work finally impress the reader as more memoiristic or fictional? Having read Beard's book several
times—for pleasure and for teaching purposes—and
having plundered it for ideas useful to my own work,
I feel confident about calling it a memoir. Although
it's not as bounded by its chronological time frame
as Conroy's—Beard also presents episodes from later
(married, separated) life—*The Boys of My Youth* basically keeps faith with the suggestion of its title. Its main
energies *are* devoted to tracking the ordeals of growing up and finding a way to live happily. The book ends
with a nostalgia-laden closing of the circle that at the
same time manages to suggest that the worst hurt of a
failed marriage has been dealt with and that new experiences are in the offing.

Like *Stop-Time*, *The Boys of My Youth* is written in
distinct, largely self-contained sections. But where only
a few of Conroy's chapters could be published on their
own, nearly all of Beard's can, and most were. This tells
us a good deal about how they were conceived and

written and lends a certain credence to the reviewer's calling them stories. For while Beard seems to hew close to the particulars of her real-life events, her staging depends on artifice—mainly on braided narratives that, in their braiding, create deliberate-feeling effects that go against the baseline "this is how it was" expectation of the genre.

In quick overview, the twelve titled pieces of the book cover, not always in sequence, Beard's childhood and girlhood, her teen years, dating, snippets of married life, a gruesome mass murder that happened at the university where she was working, and the beginnings of her writing life. If the earlier sections are more clearly defined, more strictly contained in their time frames, the later ones increasingly reflect the layering of time and the powerful incursion of memory. There is nothing proportional or shapely about the whole. The reader is aware of important gaps and the deliberately wry masking of certain painful events (the breakup of the marriage is dealt with mainly by way of brash, stiff-upper-lip asides). But for all this, the book surfaces in memory as a whole, with aspects of the suppressed story of the marriage asserting their presence as a significant negative space.

Missing almost entirely from Beard's rendered scenes and situations is the reflective voice that I have suggested is the sine qua non of the genre, vital for establishing the crucial tension of perspective. But Beard's mode of presentation compensates for this; she makes up the deficit through her structural artifice of juxtaposing two or more distinct time lines to create a comparable tension of "then and now" or "then and *then*."

A good example of this—and of Beard's method in general—is found in the long essay "Cousins." Divided into nine sections of different lengths, the essay begins with what is necessarily an imagined scene of Beard's mother and aunt, both pregnant, sitting together in a rowboat, fishing. They are relaxed, dreamily irreverent, smoking their cigarettes (this would have been the bad old days). Their way of being with each other offers a preview of what their daughters, the eponymous cousins, will be like as they grow up together.

Beard's prose here is overtly lyrical, full of metaphorical fancies—"My cousin and I are floating in separate, saline oceans. I'm the size of a cocktail shrimp and she's the size of a man's thumb"—which would be outside the "reality" pale of memoir entirely were we not willing to grant that these are Beard's own fantasy projections.

The second section introduces the cousins when they are already restless and reckless young women. They are driving in the night, on their way to a bar dance, a narrative thread that will be picked up again in section four. In arranging these panels, Beard takes license in moving back and forth in time. So the third section goes back to early girlhood, as will a later section. What gives the jumbled-seeming slide show some coherence is the recurrent background glimpse of the aunts—shelling peas, dancing at a wedding, and, finally, together in the hospital room where Beard's mother is clearly dying. In this last scene they are still having their cigarettes—sneaking them from the nurses now—and still moving together in their cloud of absolute familiarity. And here Beard gets lyrical again, projecting poetically on the sisters' mind-states, creating a somewhat overblown moment halfway between dream and idealized memory so that she can complete the essay:

> My mother sleeps silently while my aunt thinks. As the invisible hands tend to her, she dives and comes up, breaks free of the water. A few feet over a fish leaps again, high in the air. Her arms move lazily back and forth, holding her up, and as she watches, the fish is transformed. High above the water, it rises like a silver baton, presses itself against the blue August sky, and refuses to drop back down.

That baton image refers back to one of the earlier sections where the cousins are seen as little baton-toting girls going to a town parade, and it is put to work both as an emblem of wishful everlastingness *and,* like the fish, as a structural reminder, a way of reinforcing the impression that things have now come around full circle.

Beard makes much use of this technique, using it as well at the book's end, where, after all of her sufferings in her marriage and her romantic adventures and misadventures, Jo Ann gets a call from a man she has met, and the surprise intrusion sets her and her visiting girlhood friend Elizabeth to remembering how they used to torment a neighbor boy by calling him on the telephone. Writes Beard: " I don't know whether to faint or kill myself. Elizabeth laughs unbecomingly. I put both hands around my neck. We do our silent screaming routine. We are no longer bored."

Instead of using the differential between the time of some event and the time of writing as a natural spur to reflection, Beard simply narrates moments from the near present and allows the gap to fill up with resonant implication. She doesn't need to suggest to us how young she was then, or how life has thwarted her expectations, or how she learned certain bitter truths—the simple adjacency of the *then* and the *now* activates these recognitions in the reader. The book has a memory-inspired structure, shuttling freely back and forth, only the process is scenic rather than meditative. Beard is not concerned, at least on the page, with figuring out how one thing influenced another. I can see how Barbara Fisher mistook these essays for stories—they lack essayistic tissue—but Beard's manipulation of counterpointed perspectives feels purposeful. The brooding that brought the pieces together is, in Hemingway fashion, left for the reader to supply.

For her part, Maureen Howard, in her National Book Critics Circle–award-winning *Facts of Life* (1978), defies most narrative and structural conventions, giving us a memoir that moves obliquely, with unexpected associative leaps, from one part of her life to another, pouncing on what to anyone else might seem details too minor and specific to bother with, though after exposure to Nabokov we should know that everything is grist for the memory mill. In spite of its idiosyncratic narrative procedure, *Facts of Life*, like *The Boys of My Youth*, ultimately leaves us with the feeling that we have been involved in an author's complex and psychologically fraught coming-of-age.

This assertively unorthodox arrangement of remembered specifics makes any satisfying summary impossible, and to attempt to extract specific narrative or thematic threads from the text would involve us in an explanatory regress that is daunting to contemplate. Still, the memoir—like Ondaatje's wildly free-form generational narrative *Running in the Family*—reminds us of the structural flexibility of the genre and deserves attention.

Howard's method is to divide her account into three

broad categories—"Culture," "Money," and "Sex"—and then to create within each category a number of titled subsections. There is no logic of arrangement, no obvious order to the subsections. It is almost as if the author were conducting one of those literary experiments favored by the French movement Oulipo, in which a writer devises and then follows out an absolutely arbitrary system, like offering a careful description of every tenth pedestrian crossing a given street, or visiting a certain park bench every day at noon and reporting on the encounters one has. Howard is not, of course, that rigidly programmatic, but there is some way in which she does seem to delight in the challenge thrown up by what can at times feel to the reader like a whimsical arrangement.

I would argue that Howard has taken this approach as a way of proclaiming her core artistic faith, which would be that all things are intricately connected, so long as imagination is there to broker the implications; and that, where one's own life is concerned, all roads lead back to Rome. Or Home. The point is that family systems are often so densely bound together that almost any episode, narrated with the proper care and accuracy, will reveal the fundamental dynamics of character and relation. This is also one of the great lessons we take from the long recursive regress of therapy, that in our actions and relationships we will play out, over and over, the same sets of themes—until, if we're lucky, there is enough critical mass of self-awareness to change the patterns.

But in childhood such self-awareness is largely undeveloped, and Howard can pick up her threads almost wherever she chooses. Her first choice seems to me brilliantly, deliberately oblique: "'Ah, did you once see Shelley plain,'" one of my mother's beloved lines, delivered on this occasion with some irony as we watched Jasper McLevy, the famed Socialist mayor of Bridgeport, climb down from his Model A Ford."

Howard does not, as we might expect, go on with the account of seeing the mayor, but instead cites some of the favored quotations used by her mother in other contexts, somehow establishing in the process not only the woman's personality, her manner, but also something of her milieu and her cultural ambition. The strangest, most peripheral-seeming opening nonetheless plunges us directly into the life of this family, as what seems at first to conjure a world of educated reference turns out instead to reveal a frustrated aspiration. But it was an aspiration that proved decisive—it helped to push Howard and her brother toward more serious artistic pursuits.

Almost right away the author makes use of the hindsight perspective—she will do this throughout as it suits her needs—to allow us a glimpse of one of the eventual outcomes of her mother's obsession. Asks Howard:

"What did it mean to her? Was my mother full of a passionate yearning like those starved women of taste who carted their pianos across the prairie?" Then: "Or did Loretta Burns [her mother] know that her chance was gone and only want those ineffable finer things for me and George?"

The questions set up a flash-forward: "There came a day when George knew who was dancing what role in which ballet that very evening up at City Center. For the pure clean line of a particular Apollo he would leave his gray basement on St. Mark's Place—burnt-out pots, ravioli eaten cold from the can, grit in the typewriter keys." Howard's is a remarkable compression of narrative, not only in the details through which we visualize the brother's life, but also in the deft collapse of time— from mother's pretentious mannerism to son's grownup life. At the same time I don't think we are expected to engage in reductive psychologizing—it seems clear from Howard's tone, from her whole nuanced mode of expression, that she understands that causality is limitlessly intricate.

I will generalize to say that the whole of Howard's memoir moves with a similar erratic-seeming purposefulness, sketching in portraits of family and others, throwing observant glances at the social world of Bridgeport, delving into family origins (though not in the beginning where you would expect to find them, but later, especially in the section called "Money"), and then, in the last section, "Sex," not writing very much about the sexy part of sex at all, but reflecting more on first adulthood, the travails of a new (ultimately doomed) marriage, and announcing the theme of the eventual writing vocation without ever really dwelling upon it.

Finally, after all this back-and-forth flashing, this condensed time-travel, Howard brings *Facts of Life* to a close. After sketching in a scene from which it is clear that her marriage has failed, that her husband loves another (a man), she quotes in full a letter written in 1943 from her father to her mother. She chooses to foreground this loving, chatty, trivia-filled document, a freeze-framed glimpse of the ordinary affectionate interchange between husband and wife, her parents, what she calls that "ill-matched pair."

At last, on the final page, with a single short paragraph—a gesture, like Conroy's, that recognizes the extraordinary power of endings—Howard brings everything back around so that her book shows itself to be a coming-of-age memoir. She writes:

> I am walking up lower Madison Avenue in an old
> straw hat, circa 1918. Yes, always the heightening. The
> last golden hour of the day. Everything is clear: the
> rose marble of the Morgan Library, mahogany bushes,

tulips on the verge. Soon to marry, I am twenty-three
years old in a blue suit, size eight. Natural time. I
hardly touch ground the last blocks to Grand Central,
but come triumphantly to rest alone on Forty-second
Street, on the edge of evening. I am beginning. My life
is beginning which cannot be true.

A most enigmatic last line, but somehow it captures
that complex and dissonant recognition—a person can
feel new, reborn, unfledged, even though the history of
her formation runs as deep as she can follow. Howard
expresses, I think, the mystery of growth and change,
confirming what we all experience throughout our
lives: a shift in perspectives draws a new circle around
what we knew and makes all things seem possible again.
Doing so she has gotten hold of some part of the es-
sence of memoir as well, suggesting how it can be both
opaquely scenic—unmediated and unmeditated—and
expressive of the referential depth of experienced time.

Beard and Howard offer very different instances of
memoir that is not only determinedly nonlinear but
is, in key ways, almost closer to collage. The reader
fills in strategic blanks with surmises and imaginings,
and at the same time keeps rearranging the narrative
furniture. The risk with collage is that while it looks
temptingly simple—much as an abstract expressionist
painting might to a first-time viewer—it requires care-

ful intuitive calibration of effects. Some juxtapositions work, others don't. Some blank spaces invite speculation, while others feel like careless omissions. There is no program for approaching the material in this way, but the writer needs to be able to step away from her material enough to measure the different possible effects, to judge structural options. This is obviously more difficult when the driving pressure is a single strong emotion. The collage effect, like revenge, is a dish best served cold.

Fathers and Sons

The long work of growing up, of slowly making a self from all the complex givens of family and circumstance, ends up being for many of us the defining narrative of our lives, one to which later relationships, or marriage, career, and parenthood form a kind of extended postscript. Although life may hold dramatic turns of every sort, few of these are more compelling than the passage into self-aware adulthood. And even if there *are* such turns—of course there are—the fact is that they almost inevitably come after; they lack the freshness and single-mindedness of the defining primary struggles. Hindsight is transformative: what felt like a murky day-to-day travail can start to look like a fate, a destiny, an intended wresting of a single outcome from many possibilities. The chaos of experience has taken on the shape of a story, the most interesting one we have to tell. Not surprisingly, the vast majority of memoirs center on this coming-of-age period.

Every person's story is unique, particular in the most unexpected ways, but even so, there are certain recurrent archetypes, including the basic permutations of what was once commonly called "the family romance." The phrase comes from Sigmund Freud and refers, in his work anyway, to the playing out of the Oedipal drama, which for him was the central development of childhood and adolescence. Put in its most lurid light, the drama expresses the deepest primitive impulses, which Freud identified as the Oedipus complex, the young male's desire to kill his father and sleep with his mother, and, reversed, the Electra complex, the daughter's longing for her father.

The Freudian concept of the family romance has fallen out of favor in recent years among psychotherapists, at least so far as the insistence of its particulars goes, but no one denies that there is no single more formative influence than the child-parent relationship.

It comes as no surprise, then, that a great many coming-of-age memoirs put some version of this relationship right at the center. What's more, all bonds, all configurations, are represented, whether it be sons writing about their mothers (Frank McCourt's *Angela's Ashes,* Paul West's *My Mother's Music,* Elias Canetti's *The Tongue Set Free,* Russell Baker's *Growing Up),* daughters about fathers (Sue Miller's *The Story of My Father,* Susan Cheever's *Home Before Dark*), daughters on mothers (Jamaica Kincaid's *Annie John,* Vivian Gornick's *Fierce Attachments,* Mary Karr's *The Liars' Club*), or sons about fathers (Paul Auster's *The Invention of Solitude,* Geoffrey Wolff's *The Duke of Deception,* Blake Morrison's *And When Did You Last See Your Father?,* Clark Blaise's *I Had a Father,* Rick Moody's *The Black Veil*).

I've named only a few examples—the genre is rich—
and each psychological configuration can be explored
at depth. For my purposes, because my interest lies less
in psychology here than in strategies of presentation—
the endlessly variable exploration of the past using
hindsight awarenesses—I will look at sons and fathers,
and then daughters and mothers (though I will also
consider, in a later section, <u>Kathryn Harrison's *The
Kiss*</u>, which treats very directly of a now old-fashioned-
sounding Electra complex). These pairings are charged
with tension and rich with theme, though the works
I read turned out to be less centered on the classic
Oedipal *agon* than I would have expected. Instead, I
found much more focus on the <u>quest for the elusive or
absent father on the part</u> of the sons, and accounts of
intense enmeshment struggles between daughters and
their powerful mothers. And while these two patterns
hardly exhaust the repertoire of possibilities, they point
us to some of the key elements of the coming-of-age
memoir—for of course these intense familial reckon-
ings can be seen as belonging to that larger category.

I begin with sons writing about fathers because it
is for me the familiar combination. My main struggle
when I was growing up was with my father, and when I
came to write my own memoir, those tensions figured
in. I tried many approaches, looking to catch the right
sense of private drama, fighting to find a balance between what felt like confessional self-exposure and a

more restrained presentation. Working this close to the source points wasn't easy. <u>I was very concerned about boundaries, hurt feelings, and violation of the codes of privacy that most families tacitly honor.</u> Confused, I searched for precedent.

But as I looked around for exemplary works—memoirs that addressed the classic struggle of wills—I found very little. In earlier periods, yes—John Stuart Mill and Edmund Gosse had both written about the core generational opposition. But turning to our own period, while there is no dearth of sons taking on the father project, I drew a blank. Had the tyrants and soul swallowers all gone away, or had they destroyed the opposition to a man? I knew that the answer was "no" to both. But for some reason the ancient conflict of wills was not provoking our male memoirists. What the sons *were* writing about, instead, were all of the absent, elusive, confoundingly inaccessible fathers. The motive seemed to be less combat or the settling of accounts than a desire for connection, for a genuine embrace that never quite happened. These writers all needed to go back over the ground of their younger years, to locate something they felt had been lost in themselves.

But while there is an essential thematic kinship in many of the works I read, different circumstances and writerly temperaments ensure that the works themselves will present the family situation in sharply original ways. The three memoirs I will discuss—Paul Auster's *The Invention of Solitude,* Geoffrey Wolff's *The Duke of Deception,* and Blake Morrison's *And When Did You Last See Your Father?*—create three utterly unique personal topographies, even as they obey similar archetypal promptings.

Paul Auster's *The Invention of Solitude* is the least overtly memoiristic of the three. Comprising two separate sections, written at least a year apart, using distinctly different authorial voices, the book still pushes for a basic unity. The sections, each made up of compressed panels (not unlike the short sections that Woolf uses in "A Sketch of the Past"), fit together because the framing situations are in chronological sequence and because a similar pressured intensity runs through both. We read them as bulletins from an anguished period in Auster's life.

The first section, "Portrait of an Invisible Man," is Auster's brooding reflection on the father he scarcely knew. Dated simply "1979," the work is directly occasioned by the man's death and the memories and pangs of absence that haunt him in the weeks that follow. The other section, "The Book of Memory," is dated "1980–1981." This is a notebook of meditations organized according to certain key motifs—commentaries of "the nature of chance" (a central Auster topic), explorations

of specific memories, and various musings on Carlo
Collodi's *The Adventures of Pinocchio,* in particular
the father/son symbolism. As the implicit frame of the
first section was the time period following the father's
death, so "The Book of Memory" unfolds as Auster,
now separated from his wife and young son, lives by
himself in a small room in New York. The author has
abandoned the first-person voice for a fashionably ini-
tialed third person: he calls himself "A.," though whether
this is meant as a distancing or a universalizing conceit
is not quite clear.

Reading *The Invention of Solitude,* we inevitably
wonder about the elasticity of the genre. How does this
peculiar mélange of reflections earn its "memoir" tag?
Auster tells us very little about his own life, really—there
are few growing-up anecdotes and whatever tensions
get generated are more philosophical than narrative. The
answer lies in the unstated—in the "white spaces." For
even though we are told only the most selective details
about Auster, his past or his present circumstances, the
bits we *are* given are curiously amplified by the sequence
of his reflections no less than by their philosophical texture. Auster creates the white spaces, the eloquent gaps,
that invite our speculative attributions. In the context
he provides, a single image from his solitary childhood
allows us to suppose whole kindred scenarios. We finish by believing that we know a good deal about the

How is this memoir?

sketched-in life. Equally interesting, the two sections of the book work together after the fact to create a psychological portrait of Auster. Our emerging sense of the man—as son, as father, as writer—compensates for the lack of much overt narrative tension.

Even though the narrative component is minimal, "Portrait of an Invisible Man" has the feeling of an existential detective story, not unrelated to the atmospheres he created fictionally in the books of his early *City of Glass* trilogy. "The news of my father's death came to me three weeks ago," writes Auster, adding just a few sentences later: "I could not muster a single ennobling thought." He clarifies his reaction somewhat by offering a summary characterization of the man: "Devoid of passion, either for a thing, a person, or an idea, incapable or unwilling to reveal himself under any circumstances, he had managed to keep himself at a distance from life, to avoid immersion in the quick of things. . . . Death has not changed anything."

my dad

It is hard to imagine a less promising subject for a memoir than an absence, a nonrelationship, but Auster is able to take this least promising premise and give it a philosophical tilt. He makes his text an investigation of the mysteries of identity and relationship, and in the process exposes a good deal about himself—the wounded son who inherited little more than his memories of a life-sized absence.

Out of this lack—and we see this so clearly in this little book—grows the compensatory impulse to forge connection through words, to make art. Auster's own description of his feeling catches the tormented urgency that underlies this memoirist's enterprise:

> There has been a wound, and I realize now that it is very deep. Instead of healing me as I thought it would, the act of writing has kept this wound open. At times I have even felt the pain of it concentrated in my right hand, as if each time I picked up the pen and pressed it against the page, my hand were being torn apart. Instead of burying my father for me, these words have kept him alive, perhaps more so than ever. I not only see him as he was, but as he is, as he will be, and each day he is there, invading my thoughts, stealing up on me without warning: lying in the coffin underground, his body still intact, his fingernails and hair continuing to grow. A feeling that if I am to understand anything, I must penetrate this image of darkness, that I must enter the absolute darkness of earth.

In some ways, then—and this was certainly my own experience—memoir is undertaken not just as another kind of artistic expression, which is to say a work created for an intended audience, but also as an act of self-completion. The writer discovers that fashioning a narrative from memory can be an occasion of emotional return, creating a connection that was perhaps missing in the experience itself. It can be restorative, compensatory in the deepest way.

The intensity of Auster's tone here is very much at odds with the coolness of other passages, where we can almost picture the author as a forensic specialist, touching the evidence at the crime scene with a pointer: "What is one to think, for example, of a closetful of clothes waiting silently to be worn again by a man who will not be coming back to open the door? Or the stray packets of condoms strewn among brimming drawers of underwear and socks? Or an electric razor sitting in the bathroom, still clogged with the whisker dust of the last shave?"

Much of "Portrait of an Invisible Man" transmits this distanced, stricken wondering, this sense of a mind sifting through its sparse memories, as well as the literal remains of a life, in an effort to find what it knows cannot be found—the spirit of a man. And even in the hands of a speculative intelligence like Auster's, the material could begin to seem thin. There are only so many ways to repeat the question: "What kind of a man was he?" But Auster has a surprise to spring. Among the relics he finds as he sorts through his father's things is a photograph, a family portrait from when his father was but a year old. Close inspection reveals a tear and a repair, and then—entirely unexpected—evidence that a figure has been cut out of the photograph. His grandfather is missing.

This discovery is all the pretext Auster needs for recounting, in fairly abbreviated fashion, the family tragedy. "My grandmother murdered my grandfather. On January 23, 1919, precisely sixty years before my father died, his mother shot and killed his father in the kitchen of their house on Fremont Avenue in Kenosha, Wisconsin." For a few pages he reports such details and suppositions as survive in old newspaper clippings.

But Auster does not, as another writer might, turn the sensational situation into a narrative centerpiece; nor does he go on to psychologize what effect the tragedy might have had on the then-young boy. Instead, trusting that the reader will deduce and impute, filling in these blanks as well, he continues on with his otherwise nondramatic reflection.

trust the reader's intelligence to deduce

Auster makes a smart move, I think. For we do, whether we ought to or not, grant the account, the real-life facts of it, a powerful explanatory power. With no coaching from the author, we connect the absence of the father and the long-term impact of the murder; we give the tragedy a causal bearing through time and trace the ripples into Auster's childhood, then go even further, linking the loss, the wound, as directed, to his writing of the text we are reading. But the literary deed is not the end of this chain of effects. For as Auster draws this section to a close, he brings the focus of attention around to his own young son, "the image of his sweet and ferocious little body, as he lies upstairs in his crib asleep." With this the line of narration bends around into a circle. The implication I draw is that his own love and attention, prompted by this deepest need, will express itself and begin to reverse the cycle.

But if this seems too clear a resolution, the second section, "The Book of Memory," throws us back into anomie. Only now Auster is the third-person "A."—and it's not clear what has dictated this strategy. He stays true to the particulars of his own autobiography. His father has recently died. Separated from his wife and their young son, he lives in Paris alone, brooding and writing. But just as the revelation of the murder becomes a kind of explanation of the father's lack of affect, so the absence explored in the first section has conditioned our sense of the author. Reading of his solitude, his depressive conjectures about episodes from his past, we filter these through what we know of his circumstances growing up, filling in the basic causal sequence. How else do we catch hold of a passage like the following, on the particular pressure that its present-tense vantage point puts on the different layers of past that we've been tracking?

> A man sits alone in a room and writes. Whether the book speaks of loneliness or companionship, it is necessarily a product of solitude. A. sits down in his own room to translate another man's book, and it is as though he were entering that man's solitude and making it his own. . . . A. imagines himself as a kind of ghost of that other man, who is both there and not there, and whose book is both the same and not the same as the one he is translating. Therefore, he tells himself, it is possible to be alone and not alone at the same moment.

This conjectural sketch, this filling of narrative blanks with surmise, is what links the otherwise disparate sections of the book and encourages us to see it as a single entity. While it is not centered enough on narrative to make it representatively a "coming-of-age" work, there is a kind of psychological closure that makes it clear the writing and completion mark a distinct stage in Auster's evolution.

In the last pages, A. reports: "That night, for the first time in his life, he dreamed that he was dead. Twice he woke up during the dream, trembling with panic." In the first part he is being directed to get into a coffin. In the second he negotiates with his ex-wife about the completion of his "Book of Memory," asking her to give it to his son after he is gone. Then he narrates a scene back in the hospital where he needs to bid farewell to his oldest friends, which he does with tears streaming down his cheeks. This dream is abruptly followed by an excerpt from a letter written by Nadezhda Mandelstam to her missing husband, the poet Osip Mandelstam, who has been taken away by Soviet authorities. Hers is a document of the most forlorn, profound longing, a cry of love that recognizes futility even as she asserts her sorrow: "You are with me always, and I who was such a wild and angry one and never learned to weep simple tears—now I weep and weep and weep . . . It's me: Nadia Where are you?" Significantly, this is the strongest overtly expressed emotion in the book; it works by proxy, underscoring for us the author's own inability to vent his own feelings.

Although Auster's emotional process is presented only in these indirect—but saturated—bits, we feel that something very deep and painful has been gone through. His writing now seems like a rededication, a craft undertaken in full recognition of loss and emptiness. We know that a rite of passage has ended, that the writer has survived.

There are so many ways in which Auster's memoir goes against the commonsense rules of the genre. For one thing—and it's hard not to sound like a teacher here—it tells much more than it shows. I don't mean to suggest that there are authorized proportions, there aren't. But from the point of view of the reader, telling is a much harder sell. Those of us turning the pages crave pictures and scenes; we want the feel and look of things, and we grow impatient if we have to read for too long without contact with the grain of the real. Or, I would add, without any significant psychological suspense. That Auster keeps a reader in his grip finally testifies to the force of his singular intelligence, to the fact that the reader wants to experience the assaults of the real through his sensibility. If there is a lesson to be extracted, it would be the one expressed in the famous Mies van der Rohe formula: "Less is more." The eloquence of the unstated should not be disregarded, the more so as one of the besetting temptations of the genre is filling in, telling more than is necessary. *The Invention of Solitude* reminds us of the power of the other possibility.

One of the intriguing anomalies in the contemporary literary world has been the appearance of distinctive coming-of-age accounts by Geoffrey and Tobias Wolff, brothers separated at a fairly young age by divorce. Geoffrey, the elder, was raised by his father, an experience intense enough to occasion *The Duke of Deception: Memories of My Father*, while Toby, in his mother's custody, endured the brutality of his stepfather, Dwight, and chronicled their struggle in his *This Boy's Life*. In each work we catch distant glimpses of the other brother and parent. This is finally the main linking thread between the works, for in other respects they are very different, not only in terms of situation depicted, but also in mode of presentation.

Geoffrey's memoir, more complex in its weave, lends itself better to the discussion of fathers and sons. While *This Boy's Life* does express the pitched struggle of wills I was searching for, Dwight is more a simple adversary than a classic father figure. The all-important genetic connection is missing.

Similarities between Auster's account and Wolff's, though few, are instructive where they occur. Both memoirs, for instance, begin with news of the father's death, allowing the authors to propose an essentially circular narrative strategy. The end is known, suspense is not an issue, and both are free to give their accounts in the retrospective mode. It is a purposeful strategy. Where closure is implicit, there is great freedom to work speculatively and anecdotally. At the same time, the vital double vantage point is a given, with any reporting of the *then* clearly originating in hindsight, a product of the writer's *now*. Very few memoirs, incidentally, are premised on the kind of narrative suspense that is so central to fiction. If outcomes are not in every case signaled early on, we are nevertheless always aware that the subject has survived to tell the tale—which is a given only in first-person novels.

Wolff's decision to begin with the fact of the father's death also carries the subliminal sense of "now, at last, this can be told." The reader trusts that <u>the death has</u> <u>not only closed off the story but that it also likely al-</u> <u>lows for a greater objectivity of disclosure;</u> although, of course, no child's account of life with a problematic parent will ever finally be disinterested.

Wolff uses the opening scene to create a sense of mystery, not quite like Auster's, which is existential—"what can be known of the life of a man?"—but psychological, as will befit his subject. The author is visiting at the home of his wife's grandmother in Narragansett, Rhode Island, when a relative takes a phone call and comes to him with the news that his father has died. Wolff sets the moment up with a storyteller's sense of suspense:

John said: "Your father is dead."
   And I said: "Thank God."
   John recoiled from my words. I heard someone
behind me gasp. The words did not then strike a blow
above my heart, but later they did, and there was no
calling them back, there is no calling them back now.
All I can do now is try to tell what they meant.

Wolff's opening, while obviously very different, follows the same structural logic as Conroy used with the night-driving scene. He creates a time frame, a platform outside the main narrative, *and* he introduces suspense, promising a certain dark revelation even as he creates the eventual possibility of closure. Indeed, as Conroy finishes *Stop-Time* by returning to the Jaguar speeding through the English countryside, so Wolff will return to the Narragansett house when his telling is done.

His mystery—to return to the Auster comparison— is psychological. On the obvious level, we ask: "Why would Wolff respond like this?" But in a deeper way, the whole account is a kind of extended, at times anguished, marveling at the strangeness of this dangerously driven man. Auster had next to nothing to go on—his father was, as he named him, an "invisible man." Wolff, by contrast, has a superabundance of material. His father, Arthur, known to all as "Duke," was, as the moniker suggests, larger than life. Only not in a heroic way, but with a dark twist. He was, top to bottom, start to finish, a deceiver, a liar, a con man.

Wolff can't resist a few staged flourishes to introduce his father, and his point. Rather than just announcing what will soon enough be overwhelmingly obvious, he creates a seduction routine. First: "My father, called Duke, taught me skills and manners; he taught me to shoot and to drive fast and to read respectfully and to box and to handle a boat and to distinguish between good jazz music and bad jazz music. . . . His codes were not novel, but they were rigid, the rules of decorum that Hemingway prescribed. A gentleman kept his word, and favored simplicity of sentiment; a gentleman chose his words with care, as he chose his friends." And so on. Then: "After Yale—class of late nineteen-twenty something, or early nineteen-thirty something—my father batted around the country, living a high life in New York among school and college chums, flying as a test pilot, marrying my mother, the daughter of a rear admiral. . . . Later he transferred to the OSS, and was in Yugoslavia with the partisans; just before the Invasion he was parachuted into Normandy, where he served as a sapper with the Resistance, which my father pronounced *ray-zee-staunce*."

He takes considerable care to set us up with an appealingly detailed and credulously presented portrait of his father—several pages worth—and then, with no warning, he punctures the whole pretense. All it takes are three quick jabs of the pin: "A pretty history for an American clubman. Its fault is that it was not true. My father was a bullshit artist."

With this, things get interesting. Now we have our first inkling of what that "Thank God" was about. What's more, we are provoked, enlisted, on two different levels as readers. On the one hand we are intrigued by the man himself—outsized, compulsive, clearly a character. On the other, we can't help but wonder at the author's experience. What was his life with his father like that he should be so relieved to hear of his death?

Wolff lets us know right away—the passage that recalls Auster's pained admission about his need to write—just how seriously he takes his project. "In writing about a father," he asserts, quoting a letter from a friend of his, "one clambers up a slippery mountain, carrying the balls of another in a bloody sack, and whether to eat them or worship them or bury them decently is never cleanly decided." It doesn't get any more visceral than this.

Yes, the mountain is slippery. But we see just *how* slippery in the pages that follow as Wolff tries to both give an account of Duke and to write the story of his own coming-of-age. Like the other memoirists, he seeks out the balance between sustained narrative immersion in scenes of the past and the hindsight interpolations that allow us to consider the information in a larger frame. He is, in other words, creating and puncturing illusion, trusting after every deflation that the fundamental momentum of the story will pull the reader back in. The alternation neatly mimics the way we work to sustain our illusions in the face of contrary evidence.

In *The Duke of Deception* the hindsight explanations and corrections are especially important, for as readers we need to endure the same cycle of repetitions he did, accepting the con—believing that this time Duke will be true to his word—and then taking the slap of realization. Wolff refrains from using the larger hindsight perspective in order to keep his narration closer to the immediate vicissitudes of the relationship.

At one point, for instance, Duke lies to a friend of his, claiming that he knows how to sail so that the friend will give father and son the use of his sloop. Geoffrey, unsuspecting, is thrilled. But then, for three days of perfectly clear weather, Duke uses only the five-horsepower outboard, never unfurling the sails. When Geoff asks why, Duke replies that the halyard is broken.

> When we returned the boat to Pinchot he asked how everything had gone, and my father said "aces." Later, in the car, I asked my father why he hadn't mentioned Pinchot's broken halyard, and he said he had fixed it.
>
> "Why didn't we sail, after you fixed it?"
>
> My father said nothing, and I understood that I had asked the wrong question. I searched this experience to unriddle what I had said wrong, but couldn't puzzle it out. It never occurred to me that my father lied.

This happens early. Over the years Duke's deceptions get more elaborate, first shading the edge and then stepping directly into illegality. There are serious ethical breaches, lost jobs, and then criminal scams buying and selling cars bought with bad checks.

His son can no longer claim innocence. His way of coping, for years, is through emulation. When Duke, who was himself bounced out of one boarding school after another, cons his son's way into Choate, Geoffrey begins his own long slide into dissipation and deceit—hanging out with a fast crowd, drinking, courting ruin. The pattern will continue even after he somehow manages to get into Princeton. Debts, threats of expulsion, broken promises.

Father and son, we see, are on a parallel track, merging their profiles:

> I drove the Porsche flat out along Nod Hill Road, just as my father drove his Ferrari . . .
>
> One night, with fog drifting across Nod Hill Road, my father and I nearly hit head on. We were drunk, and just managed to nose our cars into opposite ditches. We met in the middle of the road at the sharp right-hander near the wall of a sheep pasture and hugged and laughed.

While it's true that the contemplation of tandem dissipation, the son's in part occasioned by the father's botch of his responsibilities, would by itself compel us with its pathos, it wouldn't finally give us the closure we need for a satisfying work of memoir. Some recognition or turnaround moment is needed—not only for the full narrative satisfaction, but also to make good on the psychological suspense of the opening.

This is no small thing. A memoir, like any other work of literature, makes clear from the outset what its stakes are. We know if we are signing on for an intense psychological drama or a more bemused or speculative sort of account. [Where there is drama, as here, the author needs to bring things around so that the main tensions have been discharged and the reader feels that a passage has been fully undergone.] This requires the kind of immersed narrative engagement that is best achieved through strong scene creation.

The turning point comes when Geoffrey goes abroad for a year, to England, taking himself out of the immediate sphere of Duke's influence. He begins to discover his literary ambitions, and then returns, ready to begin his first semester at Princeton. There will be significant setbacks and crises, but his separation has clearly begun; he is on a recovery track. Duke, meanwhile, continues to decline. Unregenerate, trapped in his own cycle, he has separated from his well-to-do second wife, acquired more debt, and deepened his addictions; he finally ends up on the West Coast. He is broke, desperate, and as his behavior becomes more maniacal, his son is less and less able to help him. Fittingly, Geoffrey now gets much of his information about Duke second-hand. Later, as Geoffrey marries and begins a teaching and writing career, the two pull even further apart. Where there is no basis for communication, the options soon dry up. The estrangement deepens right up to the end: "But now he is dead, and he had been dead two weeks when they found him. And in his tiny flat at the edge of the Pacific they found no address book, no batch of letters held with a rubber band, no photograph. Not a thing to suggest that he had ever known another human being." I can't help but think of Auster's account of his father's death in "Portrait of an Invisible Man."

It may be inevitable that the experience of loss, and the intense accompanying recognition of what was never *had*, should turn a man, a father, toward his own son—in compensation, and also to look to secure the very connection that he'd missed with his own father. Wolff's response when he learns of Duke's death—the closing scene of the memoir, connecting back with the opening section—is to drive in the night to visit his friend Kay, whose husband, a friend, had years ago committed suicide. Pain is the link. "The morning with Kay changed me," he writes. "She spoke of her dead husband and I told of my dead father." Kay is the one who turns Wolff from his refusal to the acceptance he needs to find. The self-reckoning is telescoped. When he has had his talk with Kay, quite suddenly recovering the feelings that lay buried under all of Duke's lies and betrayals, he is ready to come to terms: "I had forgotten I loved him, mostly, and mostly now I missed him. I miss him." He drives back to the Narragansett house, to his wife and sons. Entering the boys' room, he makes the needed contact: "I crawled in bed beside my sweet Nicholas and took him in my arms and to began to rock him in time to Justin's regular breaths. . . . I rocked him in my arms till light came down on us, and he stirred awake in my arms as I, in his, fell into a sleep free of dreams."

Perhaps without meaning to, Wolff has enacted in his memoir a psychotherapeutic breakthrough, speaking his deepest grief to his friend Kay, connecting through her pain to his own, and then acting upon his recognition, bringing it into his life as a changed behavior, an emotional expressiveness that doesn't in any sense cancel what he has suffered, but that puts it to work, directs it.

Memoir is sometimes accused of being self-involved or narcissistic, a glorified version of what goes on in the therapist's office, where old stories are told, grievances are aired, and self-examination is carried on. There are certain commonalities, to be sure, but with a public form like the literary narrative the merely private reference has to be presented in such a way that the universal structure of the event or situation is clear. Wolff's realization, his turn toward his own sons, is given a dramatic momentum; it is shaped in such a way that the reader can connect through some comparable personal moment, some occasion when intense sorrow served as a sudden reminder of all that is precious and requires her love.

On another level, the structural logic of memoir can, as we will see, echo the long-term process of a therapy. Where the narrator presents him- or herself as confused, uncertain of outcomes—where the hindsight perspective is used only sparingly—the odds are good that the work will culminate in some breakthrough, some scene that represents realization and acceptance, which are both, of course, goals of psychotherapy. The vital difference, aside from the recasting of events in a nonprivate idiom, is that the writer must sit in both chairs, digging up the materials *and* guiding their expression, giving them form.

Blake Morrison's relationship to his father, also named Arthur, was not nearly as distanced or fraught as what Auster and Wolff experienced. Their tensions are of the more familiar, domestic sort, falling well within range of normal, so much so that one might fairly ask just how much drama or conflict is necessary for a memoir, or, turning the question around, how little is enough? My own sense is that the interest lies not in the objective scale of the outer circumstance, but in the focus and intensity with which the writer discloses the terms of mattering. Done right, the death of a family pet (I'm thinking of E. B. White's well-known essay "Killing the Pig") can be as moving as some cataclysmic reversal in the life of a monarch. All human situations have their own scale of importance, and each, taken from the right perspective, can affect a reader deeply. The trick is to find the approach that works.

For this reason I was especially fascinated by *And When Did You Last See Your Father?*, subtitled *A Son's Memoir of Love and Loss,* where Morrison combines the account of the last months in his father's life—the visits to the hospital, then the sickroom—with flashback chapters that take us through the years of his growing up. Obeying no chronological sequence, following the associative movements of memory, these chapters explore a son's complicated relationship with a difficult man. The design works. For while neither the description of the visits nor the flashback scenes are in themselves particularly arresting, in combination—moving us from one level to another, back and forth—they create a convincing portrait of the dynamics of memory. Morrison captures how it feels to try to balance our conflicting emotions about a parent, suggesting both how relationships grow and change over time as well as how we come to terms and achieve mutual forgiveness.

At the same time, Morrison's memoir is a beautiful demonstration of the two essential time lines braiding. Not only does each shift from present to past, or past to present, intensify our sense of subjective dimension, but the shifts, one after the next, give us a simulation of change and growth. In other words, this is not simply a to-and-fro pattern, but something closer to a dialectical movement. We have two representations, interwoven, synchronized, one reflecting a growth over time (the son's), the other mapping decline and death. It is a case of structure closely serving the thematic content, giving it shape and emphasis. We found a similar pattern of crossing trajectories in the later pages of *The Duke of Deception*, where, as Geoffrey gradually came into his own, Duke's life unraveled. The difference would be that where Wolff's father's collapse becomes a cautionary tale of the misused life, Morrison's finally testifies to the survival of a certain ornery dignity.

Arthur Morrison is a character not to be denied, and Morrison begins his account with a vignette that not only gives us a sharp taste of the man's personality but also the son's shame. The reader coming to this memoir on the heels of Wolff's might at first shrug—so different is the scale of offense—but part of the power of any good writer is that he creates right away his own scale of mattering. True, there are no crimes, no wound-dealing betrayals here, just a sample of fairly ordinary family life. But within the scope of expectation the achieved effect is as memorable as anything in Wolff or Conroy.

The opening scene is a flashback—a significant narrative decision, for it introduces us right away to the larger panorama of Morrison's family life, affecting us much differently than would a hospital-scene opening. Since the book began this way, we are forced, when we reach the second chapter, to register the feeling of precipitous decline; the effect could not be achieved if the sequence were reversed.

"A hot September Saturday in 1959, and we are stationary in Cheshire." The family is trapped in a long line of cars waiting to get into the lot for the Gold Cup car races. Arthur Morrison is growing ever more restless. "In the cars ahead and behind," writes the author, "people are laughing, eating sandwiches, drinking from beer bottles, enjoying the weather, settling into the familiar indignity of waiting-to-get-to-the-front. But my father is not like them." And indeed, when he can't stand it any longer, after he has fidgeted and fumed, gotten in and out of the car several times, Arthur, who is a doctor, strings his stethoscope over the mirror and pulls out of line. "'Point to the stethoscope, pet,'" he instructs his wife, and while the others in the family shrink down in their seats, mortified, he pushes to the front. There he not only bullies the gate steward into letting him into the lot, but manages then to get most of the group in without paying the entry fee. "He was not himself up to being criminal in a big way," remarks Morrison, "but he was lost if he couldn't cheat in a small way: so much of his pleasure derived from it. I grew up thinking it was absolutely normal, that most Englishmen were like this."

We know the terms right from the start. Events are not likely to be on a tragic scale. Our subject is just an ordinary human being—petty, self-aggrandizing, and not above a small scam. Clearly, the son is not portraying the father sympathetically. Our initial impulse is to be aggravated by his presumption, to dislike the man. True though this may have been of Morrison's perception, it is also strategically essential. For a good part of the final emotional effect of the book derives from the reversal of reconciliation that comes at the end. We need to have shared the son's critical "take" in order to be engaged by the transformation.

The tone has been set, and the challenge as well. How will the author create an engaging, illuminating narrative from such humble materials? Morrison trusts to the middle way—slow, nondramatic—nudging everything slowly into motion with the second chapter: "He is sitting on the far side of the bed, or someone is, someone in a thin green gown, not at all like him." But this opening sentence is deceptively loaded: indeed, considered closely it can be seen as a kind of key to the book's underlying psychological premise. We should never underestimate the power or effectiveness of even the simplest first impression. It is far easier to plant an image, a sensation, than it is to reverse or alter it with corrections. As the opening flashback offered us a sharp impression of a puffed-up and manipulative man, this beginning straightaway establishes estrangement, an incidental—but in fact essential—lack of recognition: the son's failure to take in who his father has become.

We have to wait until the very last chapter to discover why the book is titled as it is. "And when did you last see your father?" is a question put to Morrison after the death by his therapist, and what the author does, in effect, is to look past the literal intent, asking himself instead: "When did I last see the man I recognized as being my father?" Which question, pursued philosophically, becomes, as in Auster's work, "Who was the man?" and "What was he to me as a father?" In one sense, then, the whole of the memoir is the story of Morrison looking for the true answers. And once again—by now it has the status of a tried-and-true memoiristic device—we find the structuring logic of the crossing trajectories. For as the sections set in the near present show a man rapidly losing the connection to his life, to his defining habits, a man who is every day less the person his son has known, the interspersed memory chapters give us a son pushing to attain some measure of independence.

What Morrison narrates, mainly, are episodes of disaffection, scenes in which Arthur quite characteristically insists on his way, ignoring the claims and desires of all others. There is the failed camping trip, pursued in spite of soaking rain; the family ski vacation during which Arthur spends the whole time brazenly flirting with the young tour representative; and then there is Beaty, the "other" woman, with whom Arthur all but carried on with under everyone's noses, and who is revealed after Arthur's death to have been nearly a second wife to the man.

Reading, it's hard to square Morrison's recollected adolescent fury with the anxious care he (and his mother) now show for this failing figure. But that's just the point: between the evidence of failings and the sense of sorrow, the facing-up to imminent loss, we are hit with the irrational force of family love. He was a petty tyrant, yes, a foolish man in many ways, but as he edges toward death, his flawed humanness comes increasingly to the fore, to some degree revising the long history of family frictions. In the process, although we've hardly seen it happen, Morrison has come through the many stages of his alienation and has discovered acceptance, in the process facing up to his own grandiosity and pettiness. As readers we have been shuttling back and forth between two different narrative planes, each with its own emotional tonality. And accustomed as we are to juggling different perspectives, we are nonetheless subliminally affected: the former and present-day perspectives abrade in a way that helps us to accept the nature of Morrison's own inner struggle to come to terms. Ultimately, because it is our last exposure, the reconciliation story subsumes the earlier, more disaffected scenes.

That acceptance arrives with measured steps. First come all the encounters with the fact of his father's rapidly failing health, the various bodily indignities; it is a long time before the breath finally stops and just the body remains. But it happens, almost as an anticlimax. "He is dead," writes Morrison, "and I feel an odd triumph about it. He is dead, the thing (when I was small) I used to dread more than any other, but I'm still here, my mother's still here, I can hear her breathing, the world has ended but we've survived, we're OK."

At the funeral Morrison wears his father's clothes— "how well they fit me now"—and after that there is the wake, yet another stage of coming to terms. But the question posed by the therapist is the one that haunts him, and Morrison uses it to get to his final scene, the memory he will offer to sharply counter the opening memory of Arthur's irritating selfishness and pettiness— that will, in effect, declare that emotional closure has been achieved.

Morrison builds the scene by recalling an episode of recent vintage. It comes at a point when Arthur's health is already failing, but he hasn't yet taken to bed. Instead, he has insisted on coming to help his son fix up his new home. Partly this is out of duty, and manly pride, a love of tinkering, but there is also a sense that without his help the son would make a mess of things. The men work together, putting up a curtain pole, then assembling and hanging a chandelier. The scene is full of potential resonance and Morrison doesn't pretend to sidestep the symbolic aptness. But at the same time he knows to undercut the moment of triumph with a bit of the understated ordinariness that the English specialize in:

> We turn the light on, and the six candle-bulbs shimmer through the cage of glass, the prison of prisms. "Let there be light," my father says, the only time I can ever remember him quoting anything, though I can recall some joke he used to tell, about failed floodlights at Turf Moor, a visiting Chinese football team, and the punch-line "Many hands make light work." We stand there gawping upwards for a moment, as if we had witnessed a miracle, or as if this were a grand ballroom, not a suburban dining-room, and the next dance, if we had the courage to take part in it, might be the beginning of a new life. Then he turns the switch off and it's dark again and he says: "Excellent. What's the next job, then?"

It is the most domestic of moments, almost nothing has happened, but Morrison's portrayal of the man has been so honest, and the situational context so affecting, that even this most understated reflex comment takes on grandeur.

In some ways the discovery of powerful effects in seemingly small events and causes requires greater artistry than the management of full-scale crises. For everything depends on context, the creation of atmosphere, and the placement of surface nuances in such a way that their deeper implications will come clear. By itself the father's "'What's the next job, then?'" is a bland bit of patter. But coming after we have learned the whole long history of repressed affection and bluster, and their mutual efforts to puncture this, it is dense with implication and almost painfully evocative.

These three memoirs all testify to a common—possibly universal—motivation: sons needing to discover their fathers and in the process to reconcile with them. In each case closure, or roundedness, the signature move of the coming-of-age memoir, is achieved with some gesture made toward continuity. Auster and Wolff both turn—in thought, in fact—to their own young sons, while Morrison connects with the ongoingness of work; Arthur's mention of the next task reminds us that the business of living never simply stops, that commemorative pauses are simply that—occasions for remarking meaning, personal or shared. Each memoir finds a way to embody the recognition of growth. A difficult father is accepted and mourned, and then, at last, the son steps into his place. The memoir is the record of the psychological process that allowed this to happen, and as such it is a record of achieved reconciliation. To invoke a psychologiocal paradigm, the authors have worked through their difficult material—their "issues"—concluding that portion of their therapy. I say this half in jest, half seriously, for there is an undeniable sense in which the process of engaging emotionally laden memories and turning them into story parallels the work done in the therapist's office, which is in so many ways a narrative process.

Mothers and Daughters

I have indicated—stressed—earlier that this is necessarily a selective exploration of mainly contemporary memoir; the examples have been chosen more with an eye to isolating various strategies of craft than to offering a comprehensive survey of the genre. Thus, I chose to look at certain sons writing about certain fathers, and bypassed altogether sons who were coming to terms with their mothers. What's more, my choice of examples had a thematic pretext, one that perhaps left the impression that sons were all, in some way, in search of their elusive male progenitors and that reconciliation and acceptance were the incentives for their writing. Obviously this is only partially representative.

In the same way, my choice of memoirs written by daughters and centered upon their mothers will propose but one central psychological situation. To be sure, there are others. But from my vantage point as a reader it seemed that the daughters who place dominant focus on their mothers in recounting their coming-of-age do so to work through complex enmeshed relationships and painful struggles for separation. Their problem is, in this case anyway, the opposite of what their selected male counterparts wrestled with. Neither elusiveness nor understanding is at issue. The mother is not hard to find—if anything, she is hard to get away from. And the dramatized presentation of the situation is necessarily very different in tone, if not approach, from what we've seen.

This is not to suggest that coming-of-age memoirs by women need to be presented as pitched generational struggles. Annie Dillard and Maureen Howard, for instance, found approaches that were more panoramic, in which the parent had a conspicuous but not dominant role. Virginia Woolf, who had a daughter's powerful attachment, was hurled into a kind of anxious free fall by her mother's death when she was still a girl; the loss created a core of longing that was channeled into a brilliant lyricism. There are no predetermined patterns. But so far as artistic motivation goes, the crisis of entanglement and the willful push for separation have to be seen as one of the central impulses in these narratives.

Of the two works I would consider here, *Annie John* by Jamaica Kincaid, and *Fierce Attachments* by Vivian Gornick, the first is not technically billed as a memoir, but insofar as Kincaid hews very near to personal experience in all of her work and adapts to her uses a classic, psychologically almost archetypal coming-of-age template, I will rankle the border police and use it in my discussion.

I don't want to sound merely capricious about this important matter of genre status. I do have a strategic reason for including *Annie John* in my memoir category, and this has to do with my idea of double vantage points. For while it is true that Kincaid's presentation does not make use—at least not overtly—of an explicit second time vantage point, she does, as we will see, deploy a retrospective narrative voice that makes clear throughout that her first-person narrator, Annie John, understands the key phases of her coming-of-age from a hindsight perspective.

But what allows me to consider *Annie John* as memoir despite the absence of a counterpoint narration—the usual sine qua non of the genre—is the fact that she has dramatized her development by implementing a series of strongly archetypal moments, and that these become, themselves, almost a reflective element. By which I mean that we, as readers, repeatedly experience a universalized recognition that plays against the specificity of the narrative situation and functions as a counterpoint in the place of a more traditional second time frame.

Annie John is a short and structurally simple work, but the ends belie the means: the book has a compression, a specific gravity, that gives it the heft in recollection of a much longer work. In part this derives from these staged archetypal encounters and in part from the emblematic simplicity of Kincaid's Antiguan setting.

Using the first person, Kincaid lets Annie John tell the story of her growing up, from the time of her early memories to the final affecting moment when the small island boat leaves the harbor and takes her away from all that she has known and out to the world where she will begin to make her own way. Stage by stage we see her coming into her own, gaining self-possession. Even if it is the most common story in the world, by presenting Annie's maturing in terms of the successive stages of her increasingly anguished separation from her mother, Kincaid generates a powerful interior drama.

Although Annie grows up with both parents—her father is benign, fundamentally sympathetic—from the first her focus is upon her mother. But, unlike what we will see in Gornick's memoir, it will be her own self-generated emotional identification that makes the struggle increasingly intense; her mother accepts the devotion without especially encouraging it.

Significantly, Kincaid does not begin Annie John's account by focusing right away on the child-parent bond, but rather with a red herring (though one that makes a certain psychological sense). Our very first glimpse is of a girl preoccupied with the question of death. "For a short while during the year I was ten," she writes, "I thought only people I did not know died."

Annie indulges her child's fascination first by studying the funeral processions to the neighboring cemetery, "small, sticklike figures, some dressed in white, bobbing up and down in the distance." Then, aptly: "My mother said that it was probably a child being buried, since children were always buried in the morning. Until then, I had not known that children died." Kincaid undoubtedly intends the symbolic resonance here, for the core drama of the story is as much about the loss of childhood as it is about the gradual dawning of adult awareness.

It is not too soon to raise the question of voice—whether there is a crucial distinction between the "I" of the novel and the "I" of the memoir. Or, to put it another way, if there is anything about Annie's narration that precludes the work being considered memoiristic. The issue is complex and delicate, and the question has no unambiguous answer. But I would argue that the difference, such as there is, is here found not at the level of the sentence, the specific expression, but rather at the deeper level of category, or genre. I mean—and this might be controversial—that this particular text could be read successfully either way. Or both ways—but only in sequence and provided that the reader is willing to make the category substitution. To decide to read it as memoir is to accept from the outset a certain transparency, to take on the conceit of essential verisimilitude and to filter all contents through that assumption. To take the other route, to read it as fiction, asks an extra step; it requires the reader to believe that Kincaid is both inventing a world and then reporting on it.

With most memoirs the issue would never come up. Most are complexly woven through with a secondary "reflective" voice—or hindsight voice—that is difficult to consider as another layer of fiction. Kincaid's refusal of most such reflection, coupled with what would seem the strongly autobiographical basis of the presentation, allows us to play with it as a hypothetical exception. The game has value insofar as it raises the question of genre in a fresh way.

Annie is death haunted, but entirely inexperienced. When their neighbor Miss Charlotte dies, she finds she has no way to imagine the fact: "I did not know what someone looked like dead." Curious, she contrives to attend local funerals, and when on one occasion she views the body of a girl her own age, the inertness of that body shocks and disorients her; she forgets the fish she was to buy for dinner. When she gets home and is reproached, she tries to lie. But her mother catches her out. "That night," she tells, "as a punishment, I ate my supper outside, alone, under the breadfruit tree, and my mother said that she would not be kissing me good night later, but when I climbed into bed she came and kissed me anyway." It is death that causes her to draw the first sketchy line of separation. Kincaid, I would note, derives subtle advantage from the tension between the limited reach of Annie's untutored, or naïve, perspective and the reader's necessarily more experienced understanding.

Annie's devotion to her mother is clear from the outset. "When my eyes rested on my father," she explains, "I didn't think very much of the way he looked. But when my eyes rested on my mother, I found her beautiful." In the time of Annie's early girlhood, she and her mother are, at least in her mind, symbiotic, and their quiet life together, working around the house, is, as she affirms, Edenic: "Sometimes she might call out to me to go and get some thyme or basil or some other herb for her . . . Sometimes when I gave her the herbs, she might stoop down and kiss me on my lips and then on my neck. It was in such a paradise that I lived." Again, it is the reader who knows that Edens require expulsions. Annie knows no such thing, yet, a divergence that generates an undertone of pathos and involves us more deeply in her fortunes.

Growth and change will not be stayed. Kincaid captures the first real hint of the eventual parting of ways by describing how, when Annie is twelve, she and her mother go to buy new clothes for her. Coming upon a piece of material in the shop, Annie says how nice it would look on both of them, to which her mother replies, "'Oh, no. You are getting too old for that. It's time you had your own clothes. You just cannot go around the rest of your life looking like a little me.'" Annie then reflects, incorporating that unobtrusive hindsight perspective, "I was never able to wear my own dress or see my mother in hers without feeling bitterness and hatred, directed not so much toward my mother as toward, I suppose, life in general."

This is Kincaid's way of incorporating reflection, deliberately not emphasizing the implicit other time frame, the perspective through which meanings are conferred. She wants to keep the illusionism intact; at the same time, she wants the narrative to preserve its simple emblematic—or archetypal—character undiluted by the very different tonality that reflection requires.

The saga of Annie's slow and painful coming-of-age is achieved, then, by the carefully situated scenes, each of which can be seen as plotting another point on the line leading to the inevitable separation. As readers, of course, we do not "plot" in the mathematical sense, but in the other: we get immersed in the full narrative situation, and we experience each next step as Annie herself did, as a transformation of her understanding of the nature of things.

Kincaid's art is to present narrative situations in such a way that they carry reflective weight. This is the power of the archetype: it allows the concrete instance to take on a perspectival presence not unlike what hindsight consideration would supply. A classic instance occurs when Annie is well into her adolescent crisis. Pausing in front of a shop's display window, she catches an unexpected glimpse of herself:

> I saw myself among all these things, but I didn't know that it was I, for I had got so strange. My whole head was so big, and my eyes, which were big, too, sat in my big head wide open, as if I had just had a sudden fright. My skin was black in a way I had not noticed before, as if someone had thrown a lot of soot out of a window just when I was passing by and it had all fallen on me. . . . Not long before, I had seen a picture of a painting entitled *The Young Lucifer.* It showed Satan just recently cast out of heaven for all his bad deeds, and he was standing on a black rock all alone and naked. Everything around him was charred and black, as if a great fire had just roared through. His skin was coarse, and so were all his features. His hair was made up of live snakes, and they were in a position to strike. Satan was wearing a smile, but it was one of those smiles that you could see through, one of those smiles that make you know the person is just putting up a good front. At heart, you could see, he was really lonely and miserable at the way things had turned out.

In the brimstone emblem of Satan—banished from heaven for his revolt—Annie finds a fit dramatic representation of her own state. At the same time she is every adolescent face-to-face with the alienating prospect of an unknown—and terrifying—new self. But here the recognition is just the beginning of a sequence of such alienating moments. The scene continues as Annie encounters a group of boys she knows, who, at just this point of her extreme self-consciousness, begin to mock her. When she returns home, she tries to cover up her shame and distress. "'Good afternoon, Mamie,'" she says. "'I have just come home from school.'" But as it turns out, her mother had been in town and had seen her with the boys on the sidewalk. She announces to Annie just how much it pains her to see her daughter "behave in the manner of a slut." This proves to be one of their turning points, for Annie quickly fires back: "'Well, like father like son, like mother like daughter,'" leading her mother to find the most hurtful words she can. "'Until this moment,'" she tells Annie, "'in my whole life I knew without a doubt that, without any exception, I loved you best.'"

The banishment has been effected—psychologically—and Annie's pain now intensifies with each new proof of their estrangement. The tension will build inexorably to crisis.

In the seventh—the penultimate—chapter, Annie succumbs to a mysterious illness that by stages becomes a kind of journey into the deepest trenches of the self. As Kincaid presents the situation, very possibly dramatizing its givens, Annie's confinement coincides exactly with the coming of a season of torrential rain. It drums down mercilessly on the galvanized roof. The world recedes—until there is just the bed, the room, the feverish girl going in and out of her dreams. The family tries medicines, special foods, healers, but nothing avails. For of course—or so we understand—this is a sickness of the soul, a crisis struggle Annie must go through if she is ever to cleanse herself of the past. And indeed, one day, after many weeks, after it has come to seem that things will never change, there is a shift: ". . . just as mysteriously as my sickness came, so it left. At the same time, just as mysteriously as the rain came, so it left."

Having gone through her literal and, in some undeniable way, symbolic crisis, her *passage,* Annie is purged—as is the reader, who has been taken through a kind of literary catharsis. She is ready to leave. The change announces itself, like many such changes, through an inward recognition. On the day she is finally able to go outside again, her mother takes a close look at her, remarking, "'Poor Little Miss, you look so sad.'" Once again, Annie cannot tell her the truth, though now the truth is what she feels, not what she has or hasn't done:

> Just at that moment, I was not feeling sad at all, I was feeling how much I never wanted to see a boy climb a coconut tree again, how much I never wanted to

see the sun shine day in, day out again, how much
I never wanted to see my mother bent over a pot
cooking me something that she felt would do me
good when I ate it, how much I never wanted to feel
her long, bony fingers against my cheek again . . . how
much I longed to be in a place where nobody knew
a thing about me and liked me for just that reason,
how much the whole world into which I was born had
become an unbearable burden and I wished I could
reduce it to some small thing that I could hold under-
water until it died.

Kincaid finds a powerful way to orchestrate her last chapter, "A Walk to the Jetty." Annie's wish has at last been granted—she is ready to bring her saga of growth and separation to its first necessary conclusion. Arrangements have been made for Annie to sail away to England, where she will study to be a nurse. Her things are packed; she is ready. There remains only the leave-taking and the walk to the boat with her mother and father. Kincaid uses the scene to let Annie make a clear-eyed inventory of the life she has lived, reflexively reviewing her primary identifications: "The sheets on my bed my mother made with her own hands. The curtains hanging at my window my mother made with her own hands." Once again, the author manipulates the perspective split between Annie and the reader. In this case, we are the ones who take in the significance of the places and associations and register the emotion, while Annie expresses only the bitterness necessary for separation:

> I don't see them now the way I used to, and I don't love them now the way I used to. The bitter thing about it is that they are just the same and it is I who have changed, so all the things I used to be and all the things I used to feel are as false as the teeth in my father's head. Why, I wonder, didn't I see the hypocrite in my mother when, over the years, she said that she loved me and could hardly live without me, while at the same time proposing and arranging separation after separation, including this one, which, unbeknownst to her, *I* have arranged to be permanent?

On the launch taking her out to the boat, Annie has a tension-heightening moment of self-doubt, but she masters this by clamping down on her emotions:

> I was seated in the launch between my parents, and when I realized that I was gripping their hands tightly I glanced quickly to see if they were looking at me with scorn, for I felt sure that they must have known of my never-see-this-again feelings. But instead my father kissed me on the forehead and my mother

kissed me on the mouth, and they both gave over their hands to me, so that I could grip them as much as I wanted. I was on the verge of feeling that it had all been a mistake, but I remembered that I wasn't a child anymore, and that now when I made up my mind about something I had to see it through. At that moment, we came to the ship, and that was that.

And to it goes with the last good-byes, the mother's tearful embrace, Annie's quick stanching of her own tears, the launch then growing small in the distance. Her childhood is ended, and the feeling is captured in the book's final sentences, where image and actuality converge perfectly:

I went back to my cabin and lay down on my berth. Everything trembled as if it had a spring at its very center. I could hear the small waves lap-lapping around the ship. They made an unexpected sound, as if a vessel filled with liquid had been placed on its side and now was slowly emptying out.

Finishing the book, we understand that this is an achieved parting, made inevitable by Annie's character and by the nature of the relationship between mother and daughter. She has freed herself into her own life, but the price of her freedom is the loss of the solace of an ongoing connection. We have not been told enough of Annie's character to fully understand her evolution. Indeed, what we know of that character we know through these emblematic moments, these turning-point struggles that feel at every moment like they have been thrust upon her from without, as if by some agency of fate. What we tend to forget in our immersion—a function of Kincaid's careful craft—is how much the moments have been edited and staged by a writer whose understandings have been acquired over time. We experience Annie's coming-of-age as a progressive sequence, but the final feeling is of a life retrospectively known and accepted. This life is at once presented and reflectively integrated, and for this reason, though *Annie John* may be dressed up as a novel, its process and final effect make it read like a memoir.

The linear simplicity of Kincaid's narration is deceptive, and the aspiring memoirist should think twice about imitating it. Direct presentation is all too often the kiss of death in memoir. Not only does it put the burden of creating tension on the story itself—and not many real-life stories are strong enough in themselves for this to work—but it invites a proliferation of explanatory detail. Kincaid avoids this by adopting an almost fabulistic simplicity of presentation, which she can only do because her account is deeply archetypal. The success of the archetypal approach, however, depends more than a little on the Antiguan setting, which functions here as an exaggeratedly simple backdrop functions in a play.

What the aspiring memoirist *can* learn from Kincaid is the use of emblematic scenes—where one spotlit moment has the effect of standing in for, or symbolizing, a whole larger situation. This is different from what we find in Auster, where we use the offered detail as a basis for filling in the blanks of the unstated. Kincaid's carefully selected stagings acquire the expansiveness of the universal. We have no real sense of missing material, just the rich reverberation of the given.

If *Annie John* is about the drama of separation, Vivian Gornick's memoir is the reverse—is, as its title *Fierce Attachments* clearly suggests, about the lifelong frictions of an enmeshed relationship. And if *Annie John* makes use of an escalating tension, building toward crisis and resolution, *Fierce Attachments* ends as it begins, with mother and daughter caught in the vast web of their ambivalent emotions. The satisfactions Gornick offers are not narrative or in any sense suspense driven—they have everything to do with the accuracy and unsparing vigor of her presentation.

Different relationships ask for different treatments. The truth about Gornick's bitterly complex give-and-take with her mother is that it is never resolved—it is more a condition than a forward-moving story—and this dictates the structure, the unconstrained movement between the past of Gornick's growing up and the relative present, and the use of both past- and present-tense voices. We are, by design, pulled into a world where the inevitable curve of growth and change—what stood out so clearly in *Annie John*—is constantly countered by an almost dreamlike sense of repetition.

Gornick establishes her open time grid and her logic of narration straightaway. She will move freely back and forth in time by way of self-contained sections of varying lengths. She sets the precedent—the terms of engagement (if not necessarily the terms of endearment)—in the first few pages.

"I'm eight years old," she begins. "My mother and I come out of our apartment onto the second-floor landing." A very short establishing anecdote follows, planting us, though only for a moment, in the present tense of *then.* The very next paragraph, however, a new section, switches tense and declares a more distanced historical perspective: "I lived in that tenement between the ages of six and twenty-one. There were twenty apartments." Again, Gornick gives us just the briefest overview, a distanced sort of summary, before the next paragraph, opening the third short section, begins: "My mother and I are out walking. I ask if she remembers the women in that building in the Bronx." And with that deliberate little feint—mother and daughter

remember those people, that place, better than anything else in their lives—we are set up. Gornick has
alerted us to the structural procedure, but also cued us
into the fact that the relationship is ongoing, the story
unfinished. The fact that the past is invoked in both
present and past tense is also telling, letting us know
that memory will be treated both experientially and
reflectively.

We have seen how often memoirists begin their work
with a short establishing scene, the point of which is as
much to supply a point (or counterpoint) of reference as
anything else. Conroy needed to introduce the adult self,
as did Wolff, and Gornick goes in the opposite direction,
invoking herself as a young girl before continuing on.
The simplest, briefest, of conjurings—and transitions—
achieve a great deal, in effect declaring the vocational
freedom to move about in time and space.

The tenement life that Gornick re-creates for us is
a world of women. The men, the husbands, are away,
working; they have almost no presence on the page and
play minor parts at best in the emotional ecology of the
place. At the center of everything—and not just because
these are a daughter's recollections—is Gornick's mother.
Opinionated, determined, assertive, willing to make her
opinions and preferences known, she is also a moral ar-
biter. Writes her daughter: "My mother had been dis-
tinguished in the building not only by her unaccented

English and the certainty of her manner, but also by her status as a happily married woman. No, I haven't said that right. Not just happily married. Magically married. Definitively married."

Interestingly, the sections dealing with Gornick's childhood are not constructed around struggle and opposition. The author places herself in an onlooker role—the objectivity equates to a kind of unformed innocence—and sets out her mother's character mainly by reporting through close-up recollections of her relationships with the other women in the house. She focuses in particular on their beautiful, high-strung neighbor Nettie, who is all but adopted by the family. The sense of struggle, and the enmeshment that creates and exacerbates it, only develops as we move from past to near present and back and start to understand the force the mother's complex personality has come to exert on Gornick over time.

The emotional balance in the Gornick household changes decisively when the father, who has been largely missing from Vivian's account, dies. Her mother, hitherto so indomitable and controlling, collapses, revealing at a stroke the other side of her nature. Grief has unmasked the tragedienne, the seemingly helpless hysteric who now all but forces her daughter to become the emotional caretaker. Writes Gornick : "I saw myself only as a prop in the extraordinary drama of Mama's bereavement. . . .

Actually I was frightened. I didn't object to being frightened. I supposed it as good a response as any other. Only,
being frightened imposed certain responsibilities. For
one, it demanded I not take my eyes off my mother for
an instant." With good reason. "At the funeral parlor she
tried to climb in the coffin. At the cemetery she tried to
fling herself into the open grave." What is a daughter, an
only child no less, to do?

The dynamic between the two becomes over time
the Catullan *odi et amo*—"I hate and I love." As Gornick
begins to grow up, exhibiting inevitable signs of independence, her mother fights harder to keep her emotional ascendancy. At one point, when Gornick, who
is reading a comparative history of love, suggests that
love is only an idea, that there is "no such thing as the
mysterious immutable being," the woman explodes:

> Her legs were off the couch so fast I didn't see them
> go down. She made fists of her hands, closed her
> eyes tight, and howled: "I'll kill you-u-u! Snake in
> my bosom, I'll kill you. How dare you talk to me that
> way?" And then she was coming at me. She was small
> and chunky. So was I. But I had thirty years on her. I
> was out of the chair faster than her arm could make
> contact, and running, running through the apart-
> ment, racing for the bathroom, the only room with
> a lock on it. The top half of the bathroom door was

a panel of frosted glass. She arrived just as I turned
the lock, and couldn't put the brakes on. She drove
her fist through the glass, reaching for me. Blood,
screams, shattered glass on both sides of the door.
I thought that afternoon, One of us is going to die of
this attachment.

That might be a bit dramatic, but we get the point.
The surprise is that Gornick does not, on leaving
home, flee to the far side of the world, like Annie John,
that she not only remains in New York but keeps up the
relationship. Chafing and bickering are her lot—she has
accepted this. Over the years she has learned to give
as good as she gets and to live by the rhythms of their
conflict, knowing that they invariably result in truce, if
not reconciliation. The bond is as deep as her life. This
scene emphasizes Gornick's changed sense of her role.
She is no longer—if she ever really was—the "neutral"
observer; she is now an engaged, at times even histri-
onic, participant.

Their cyclic struggle plays out over and over, but
not without some change and growth. We see progress, for example, in one instance where Gornick has
loaned her mother a biography of Josephine Herbst,
thinking she will admire the life. Alas, no. "'Maybe this
is interesting to you,'" her mother says, "'but not to
me. I lived through all this. I know it all.'" As Gornick

reflects: "Invariably, when she speaks so, my head fills with blood and before the sentences have stopped pouring from her mouth I am lashing out at her. . . . On and on I would go, thoroughly ruining the afternoon for both of us." But, as she then adds, allowing a flash of hope: "However, in the past year an odd circumstance has begun to obtain. On occasion, my head fails to fill with blood. I become irritated but remain calm."

Gornick chooses to offer a placating response instead of the usual bitter retort and the shift is perceptible:

> Silence. Long silence. We walk another block. Silence. She's looking off into that middle distance. I take my lead from her, matching my steps to hers. I do not speak, do not press her. Another silent block.
>
> "That Josephine Herbst," my mother says. "She certainly carried on, didn't she?"
>
> Relieved and happy, I hug her. "She didn't know what she was doing either, Ma, but yes, she carried on."

The rhythm of rage and reconciliation governs the relationship and the unfolding of the memoir, moving through right to the conclusion. But Gornick, it turns out, has alerted us to this from the very beginning. In the second short section of the book, where she is pulling back to set out the perspective, the hindsight view of life in the Bronx tenement, she writes, apropos of the women in the building:

There would be years of apparent calm, then suddenly an outbreak of panic and wildness: two or three lives scarred (perhaps ruined), and the turmoil would subside. . . . And I—the girl growing in their midst, being made in their image—I absorbed them as I would chloroform on a cloth laid against my face. It has taken me thirty years to understand how much of them I understood.

Gornick has right here captured the deep paradox at the heart of the enterprise, the inevitable tension between the distance required for apprehension—for a perspective to emerge in which events can find their proper place—and the pressured immediacy of vivid narrative. It's hardly a surprise that the memoirist looking deep into the past should find herself constantly moving between experience tasted and experience digested. Gornick shows herself remarkably adept at just this oscillation, knowing when to focus the lens and when to pull back—there is no rule book telling a writer when and how to finesse the transitions.

Gornick brings *Fierce Attachments* full circle at the end. Her fierce mother is now old—diminished, but hardly silenced. In the last scene of the memoir they are sitting together in her mother's Manhattan apartment, far from their place of origins. "Because we are silent," Gornick writes, "the noise of the street is more compelling. It reminds me that we are not in the Bronx, we are in Manhattan: the journey has been more than a series of subway stops for each of us. Yet tonight this room is so like that other room, and the light, the failing summer light, suddenly it seems a blurred version of that other pale light, the one falling on us in the foyer." Here is closure achieved through a kind of merging of past and present.

But then, lest we be lulled too much into a sense of harmony, Gornick gives us the final exchange, which so perfectly captures both the friction of two contentious natures and at the same time reminds us that this has all along been this mother and daughter's way of testing and verifying the love between them:

> My mother breaks the silence. In a voice remarkably free of emotion—a voice detached, curious, only wanting information—she says to me, "Why don't you go already? Why don't you walk away from my life? I'm not stopping you."
>
> I see the light, I hear the street. I'm half in, half out.
> "I know you're not, Ma."

Fifteen years after it was first published, *Fierce Attachments* was the occasion of a controversy in the literary world. Giving a talk on memoir at Goucher College, Gornick admitted to a questioner that certain episodes in the book were composite re-creations, true to the story, but not necessarily literal transcriptions of incidents as they happened. Her remarks provoked a mini-furor, on-site and then on the Internet, raising the question which can never be answered to everybody's satisfaction: What are the limits of invention in memoir?

Common sense tells us that not all so-called nonfiction can be—or needs to be—accountable to the same standards of strictness. Documentary reportage, kin to journalism in its treatment of character and circumstance, is pledged to absolute factual veracity, though I doubt that any work in the genre is completely free of grace notes and bits of embroidery. But memoir, a genre that not only depends upon memory, but has the relation of past to present itself as an implicit part of its subject matter, is different. So much of the substance of memoir is not *what exactly happened?* but rather, what is the expressive truth of the past, the truth of feeling that answers to the effect of events and relationships on a life? And from this angle, Gornick's conflations make sense; for she uses them to better, more truthfully (if not more accurately) communicate the essential nature of what she is after. What she is doing—heightening, conferring definition—is in some ways not so different from what writers like Nabokov or Woolf are doing when they zoom in on minute particulars to the exclusion of the more customary narrative proportions. The truth is in the specific psychic residue, not in the faithful mapping of episodes to external events.

I offer this knowing that there will be many people who disagree. But it seems to me that memoir, unlike reportage, serves the spirit of the past, not the letter. Indeed, no one who reads memoir believes—how could they?—that exchanges happened exactly as set down, or that key events have not been inflected to achieve the necessary effect. The question is only *how much* departure is tolerable, and at what point does the modified recollection turn into fiction?

My own answer has always been that the memoirist writes from a subjective provocation, following an imperative to express the true dynamics of some part of the past. The distilled experience then exists as a specifically contoured shape, the stored sensation of "how it was." This is what the memoirist seeks to reproduce. As the poet Stephane Mallarmé insisted, "Paint, not the thing, but the effect which it produces." Exactly right. And in capturing the effect the need for accuracy is absolute. The writer must represent as faithfully as possible what memory has shaped inside—memory and feeling. This, needless to say, may prove to be different in some respects from what may have been captured by an unseen crew of recording technicians. Distortion is inevitable, permissible, so long as it is in the service of the truth that overrides the literal sequence of events. I believe Gornick wrote her scenes as she did because *that* presentation and not some other held the truth she was after. This is not to say that some memoirists might not steer in the direction of effect, to up the intensity or to confer a more pleasing outline. They ask: Who will ever know the difference? Here I would only say that honesty of tone is a hard-won quality and that good readers are highly sensitive to its nuances. A memoirist takes an enormous risk when she invents or distorts for effect. False emotions have a hollow sound, and while trust is easily shaken, it is very hard to regain.

Trauma and Memory

"Traumatic memoir," if I can try out such a phrase, seems to me a distinct subgenre, in important ways allied to, but also standing apart from, works that deal with coming-of-age. Pain and psychological injury, when raised to the level of trauma, create discontinuities in a life that often require different strategies of presentation. One way to get at the difference I'm talking about is to contrast these memoirs with the lyric kind. They clearly sit at opposite sides of the spectrum. Where lyric memoirs are undertaken contemplatively, often in a spirit of curiosity, and are bent on recovering the felt core of early experience, implicitly searching out the persistence of the self over time, trauma-based accounts are very often private salvage operations. Rather than assuming continuity, they must, at the deepest level, reflect and somehow compensate for its destruction. For a trauma is a rupture, a break (literally "wound"), whether brought on by a single experience or, more commonly, the infliction of a repeated injury that cannot be integrated; the normal continuum of growth is violated. The impulse for expression is different at the very core.

Psychologists often talk of the "repetition compulsion"—the process whereby an individual keeps symbolically reenacting a distressing situation, hoping to master it, to get it right and be free of it. It's no stretch, I think, to see the work of these memoirists as a purposefully undertaken repetition, the goal being comprehension and exorcism: psychological control. However different the nature of the trauma itself—I will look at four very distinct kinds of crisis—what the writers share in common is an impulse to represent the overcoming of the wound, whether through repair, reconciliation, or redemption. And while there may outwardly not be much in common between the damage inflicted by a mother's psychotic breakdown (Mary Karr), violation at the hands of a pedophile (Richard Hoffman), severe surgical disfigurement (Lucy Grealy), and father/daughter incest (Kathryn Harrison), this drive to achieve an integrating outcome influences the shaping of the presentation in all instances.

On the most basic level, trauma-based narratives are crisis centered. The pain that leads to breakage is not only intense, it is very often situation based. Something happened—something explosive. The narrator's assumptions about the world were shattered, bringing about collapse or some other severe reaction. Eventually— and the memoir itself, the writing of it, is testament to this—some understanding or acceptance was achieved. There is a basic narrative progression that needs to be represented, though as we will see, the unique nature of each private crisis dictates equally unique approaches to solution.

I debated for some time whether to discuss Mary Karr's *The Liars' Club* with the other mother/daughter memoirs, or under the trauma designation. Certainly the complex intensity of the relationship between Mary and her mother would give the book a place right alongside *Annie John* and *Fierce Attachments.* But what I couldn't ignore as I reread the book was the governing logic of Karr's construction, which dramatized from the first page the impulse to forget the unbearable. What's more, the mother's own crisis had everything to do with the ruptures brought on by concealment and denial. Trauma in the life of the mother was inflicted, as it so often is, on the child. Or, in the words of one of Karr's favorite poets, Philip Larkin: "Man hands on misery to man. / It deepens like a coastal shelf." But this child put the puzzle together, achieving, on paper at least, a satisfying explanatory coherence.

Mary Karr did not set out to write *The Liars' Club* as a memoir—its first incarnation was fiction. I know this because many years ago the author was part of a writing group to which I also belonged. Every second Sunday in the Poetry Room of Harvard's Lamont Library, our shifting population of ten to twelve writers took turns presenting their work. In those days Karr was still casting the material of what would become her hugely successful memoir as invention. She hadn't yet seen her way clear to making the leap.

I don't know exactly how she came to the decision—certainly a number of us encouraged her in that direction before she left the group—but I do remember that as soon as I read the finished book and saw the familiar characters and episodes in a new narrative light, I understood that she had made the right choice.

In their original fictional form, Karr's alternately wrenching and comic depictions of a girl growing up in a hard-luck family in a hardscrabble East Texas town had powerful local momentum. Scene by scene they worked to great effect—Karr was no less tough, poignant, or comic than in the memoir. But set out sequentially, as parts of a longer narrative, the sections did not build to a larger defining tension. What had been missing—and this became clear right away once I read the memoir—was the mother's story, the source of the trauma that kept sending Karr back to her past. Once that trauma was revealed—*as* trauma, as wound—the complicated structural design of her memoir became possible, and with it a mode of telling that allowed her to offer her experience as a story of reconciliation, even redemption.

The Liars' Club is constructed along a twin axis, with the first part of the book revolving around the repression and eventual recovery of a traumatic memory, and the second working through the deliberate concealment and ultimate revelation of a classic "dark secret." As both center on Karr's vivid, self-destructive, episodically psychotic mother, the memoir is, in effect, a daughter's tormented working-out of that core relationship.

Karr opens with this declaration: "My sharpest memory is of a single instant surrounded by dark." Mary is seven, sitting on a mattress, while the family doctor inspects her for injuries. "'Show me the marks,'" he says. "'Come on, now. I won't hurt you.'" Something has happened, there has been violence, but we are not told what it is. And having caught her moment with flashbulb clarity, having hooked us in, Karr breaks off. "It took three decades for that instant to unfreeze," she writes. "Neighbors and family helped me turn that one bright slide into a panorama."

This first section of *The Liars' Club,* entitled "Texas, 1961," artfully flirts with disclosure, moving back and forth in time, selectively invoking perspectives of enlightened hindsight, but also holding back. Although it is just a single moment she claims to be documenting, Karr jumps forward as narrative need dictates, loosening the frame enough to lead us into her life at the time while still not tipping her hand. What provides the essential suspense is our curiosity about the yet-undisclosed information. Several paragraphs in she gives us an image that clarifies the dynamics of psychological repression: "It was only over time that the panorama became animate, like a scene in some movie crystal ball that whirls from a foggy blur into focus. People developed little distinct motions; then the whole scene jerked to smooth and sudden life."

For pages then we are in Litchfield, Texas, with Mary and her older sister Lecia and her parents, their father a rough-cut, hard-drinking oil-field worker, their mother a nervous, glamorous, and artistically ambitious woman deeply at odds with her lot in life. Karr uses a scrappy, knowing child's voice to develop vivid tableaux of the dreary, depressed town, the bar where her father and his cronies gather to swap their stories (the eponymous "liars' club"), the drinking and fighting and making up of her passionate but mismatched parents, the frightful stages of her grandmother's death by cancer. Every so often, though, Karr the grown-up narrator steps in, reminding us that we are still, on one level, inhabiting a suspended moment, and that some clarification will eventually have to be offered. "Because it took so long for me to paste together what happened," she writes, working the lever of deliberate suspense, "I will leave that part of the story missing for a while."

What she does, meanwhile, is to gradually develop the portrait of family life, in particular her mother's growing despair, so that when the moment of truth arrives we can make sense of it. To be fully effective, this despair must be intensified in a plausible way. And it is. Karr narrates fierce domestic battles, the horrific deterioration of her grandmother, and her mother's mounting rage and frustration. "Sometime after New Year's," the child voice tells us, "two bad things jump-started my parents into an evil stretch—drinking and fighting." And, staying inside the child's necessarily limited comprehension: "Nor can I figure out what exactly led to Mother's near-fatal attack of Nervous. Maybe drinking caused Mother to go crazy, or maybe the craziness was just sort of standing in line to happen." Here, as throughout, Karr achieves density of presentation by moving—and making her reader move—between psychologically differentiated frames of reference, between innocence of outlook and experienced hindsight.

The tension builds through a series of expertly managed scenes—domestic explosions, poignantly melancholy funks—until one day Mary comes home to find that something has gone badly wrong. We follow her along a path of intensifying anxiety:

> I ran through the house again then, calling out for Mother. What I found in her bathroom knocked the wind slap out of me. The big rectangular mirror over the sink had been scribbled up with lipstick of an

orangey-red color. Somebody—Mother no doubt—
had taken a tube of Mango Fandango or Kiss-Me
Peach and scribbled that mirror almost solid, so the
silver reflecting part came through only in streaks. . . .
A thin filter of fear came to slide between me and
the world. Objects in the house started to get larger
and more fluid. A standing lamp reared up at me as
I came on it.

Mary runs from place to place, finally finding her
mother in her studio, where she sits in a rocker burn-
ing papers in a cast-iron stove. This is just a prelude. In
what feels like an eyeblink the woman is dragging everything she can lay hold of outside and building a bonfire
behind the garage, putting her whole life to the match—
paintings, shoes, clothes. "She holds every dress briefly
by its shoulders like it's a schoolkid she's checking out
for smudges before church. Then one by one they get
flung away from her and into the fire. There sails my
white eyelet-lace Easter dress . . ." From the yard it's
back to the house. Lecia and Mary run to take refuge in
their room, and as they lie down on their quilt they hear
their mother rummaging through the cutlery drawer.
As the door opens and a "rectangle of light spills over
us," the drama is self-consciously cinematic:

Then a dark shape comes to occupy that light, a figure
in the shape of my mom with a wild corona of hair

and no face but a shadow. She has lifted her arms and broadened the stance of her feet, so her shadow turns from a long thin line into a giant X. And swooping down from one hand is the twelve-inch shine of a butcher knife, not unlike the knife that crazy guy had in *Psycho* for the shower scene, a stretched-out triangle of knife that Daddy sharpens by hand on his whetstone before he dismantles a squirrel or a chicken.

This is the breaking point, the child's ultimate terror. And what happens at this moment to Mary is telling, not just psychologically, but also for the construction of the memoir:

> No sooner do I choke down that scream than a miracle happens. A very large pool of quiet in my head starts to spread. Lecia's face shrinks back like somebody in the wrong end of your telescope. Then even Mother's figure starts to alter and fade. In fact, the thin, spidery female form in black stretch pants and turtleneck wielding a knife in one upraised arm is only a stick figure of my mother, like the picture I drew in Magic Marker on the Mother's Day card I gave her last Sunday.

Note throughout these passages the vivid intensity of the visual description—Karr is intent on incising these traumatic episodes on the reader's memory screen. And then, as if referring to—and ironically distorting—this very impulse, she gives us a visceral depiction of repression in action: "That's how God answered my prayers," she writes. "I learned to make us all into cartoons. . . . I lock all my scaredness down in my stomach until the fear hardens into something I hardly notice."

This hardening, this almost superhuman transformation of the immediate, is how Mary locks down, shutting out everything about the night for long decades—everything but the single memory that she preserves as the thread into the heart of the labyrinth: the memory that opens the book.

What follows from this retrieval of the traumatic memory—the second section of the book, essentially—feels narratively anticlimactic. We read of the mother's hospitalization, her eventual release, and then, jumping forward several years, Karr tells of the period of her parents' separation and divorce (the girls and their mother move to Colorado with money inherited from the grandmother) and then their eventual reunion and remarriage.

The last section of *The Liars' Club,* entitled "Texas Again, 1980," brings a grown-up Mary back from the East Coast to face her father's illness and her mother's deepening depression. The memoir starts to pull around full circle when Mary is going through an old trunk in the attic and finds a velvet box filled with wedding rings (her mother had married and divorced several times before she met Mary's father). She is shocked, but she is also finally compelled to find out the story. Writes Karr: "Truth was conspiring to assemble itself before me. Call it fate or grace or pure shithouse chance. I was being guided somehow into the chute that led down the dark corridor at the end of which truth's door would fly open." Here we see again the connection between the discipline of memoir and the long-term process of psychotherapy. Karr implies the idea of a destination, a breakthrough, a truth-recognition that might bring personal redemption (and, later, literary closure).

Now other old memories surface—for Mary, but also for the reader. Almost two decades ago, we recall, Mary's dying grandmother had told the sisters a story. The scene was vivid enough as Karr narrated it—

> After a while, she opened the small tablets on her lap, and they turned out to be dime-store brass frames around school pictures of two children, a boy and a girl. The pictures had a celery-green tint to them, like they'd been too long in the sun. "That's your sister and brother," she said. "That's Tex and Belinda."

—but as she was not ready to understand the significance, she did not linger. She and Lecia forgot, and so did we. But now, at memoir's end, the story resurfaces. It turns out to be the key to many locked-up mysteries.

When Mary confronts her mother about the rings,

when it is clear that the past can no longer be hidden and denied, the two women go out together to drink margaritas and talk. Karr narrates a tour-de-force moment in the local Mexican café as the story of the past, of the abandoned children, the guilt and misery of the loss—everything tumbles out, all of her mother's long-concealed guilt and shame, and at last the women connect with the truth. There is a palpable release of tension, though as Karr writes the scene, it will take more time—and possibly the discipline of writing itself—for her to grasp the full meaning of the afternoon's confessions:

> The sunset we drove into that day was luminous, glowing; we weren't.
>
> Though we should have glowed, for what Mother told absolved us both, in a way. All the black crimes we believed ourselves guilty of were myths, stories we'd cobbled together out of fear. We expected no good news interspersed with the bad. Only the dark aspect of any story sank in. I never knew despair could lie. So at the time, I only felt the car hurtling like some cold steel capsule I'd launched into onrushing dark.
>
> It's only looking back that I believe the clear light of truth should have filled us, like the legendary grace that carries a broken body past all manner of monsters. I'm thinking of the cool tunnel of white light the spirit might fly into at death.

Here is a perfect instance of hindsight awareness braiding together with telling of what happened, offering the satisfying—the necessary—resolution that could only come with the sufficient passage of time.

"'It all depends how deep your brothers are buried,' my father said." The year is 1984, and as Richard Hoffman's mother lies dying in another part of the house, his father, a loss-shattered man, is already thinking of burial arrangements, looking into whether his wife can be buried on top of the two sons they lost to muscular dystrophy.

Alongside writing fiction and memoir, Hoffman is a well-respected poet, and it is hard, retrospectively, not to read the father's words figuratively as well as literally. And the memoir, *Half the House,* makes it clear that however far down in the earth the brothers are buried, the sadness of their hard lives and early deaths is alive for the author.

But the terrible losses Hoffman and his family sustained are only part of the story. The memoir chronicles as well a startlingly intense—and in places graphically narrated—series of sexual violations that Hoffman suffered at age ten at the hands of his football coach. We can't read *Half the House* without wondering just how Hoffman could make his way to adulthood with any surviving faith or hope, even as the memoir consistently emphasizes individual resiliance and the possibilities of repair and restoration.

Hoffman chooses an elliptical structural format, avoiding the cleanly circular design that is one of the staples of the genre, but achieving the effect of overlap that works as a coda might. Heading each chapter with a date, he begins the memoir with two short chapters dated "1984," the year of his mother's death, before winding back to 1956, the year he was seven. From there his short, directly written chapters bump forward as follows: 1957, 1958, 1959, 1960, 1962, 1962, 1964, 1970, 1972, 1975, 1984, 1990, 1990, 1990, 1990, 1990. I apologize for listing the dates in this fashion, but to the reader looking back they compress certain significance. Even without looking back, we can see that the years of boyhood are more closely documented, that Hoffman then leaves substantial gaps of time between sections, and, finally, that there is a sustained focus on events in 1990.

The gaps prove to be as telling as the documented periods, as does the unstated: the drama of psychological consequences. Hoffman decides to present what happened with the least possible reflection or commentary. He trusts that the sketched-in effects over time will acquire the power of implication we have learned to expect from the Hemingway aesthetic of surfaces arranged to indicate emotional depths. For the memoirist this is an important early decision to make, one that determines much about the structure of the work—whether to grant to scenes their maximum power of evocation and skew the balance toward experiential immediacy, or else to make use of the full range of reflective intervention. It is the difference—to choose extremes—between a Conroy and a Nabokov. The former would underscore the power of the event or situation itself, the latter the private alchemy whereby it gets integrated into the life.

Reading *Half the House* we are at first surprised by the absence of this reflective commentary, not to mention any detailing of plausible real-life consequences. There is little dwelling on injuries sustained. Hoffman narrates the violation by the coach, or the slow death of his brother, but just when another author would linger, keeping the lens trained on the scene and trying to do justice to its full inner resonance, he moves on. Suddenly, abruptly, it is a new year, a new drama. And in the boyhood chapters there is no obvious reckoning of damage. The boy, like the rest of his family, looks to get on with things. As his mother would always say when asked how she managed all the loss in her life: "You just do it."

This seems to be Hoffman's artistic decision as well. His fast-moving early chapters enact, in effect, the common psychological reflex of denial. As Mary Karr worked the logic of repression into the very structure

Style/form
miwoing psych.
damage: repression,
denial,
blowbacks,
obsession

of *The Liars' Club*, so Hoffman builds a stiff-upper-lip dynamic of denied impacts into his book. We sense that it is not so much that the boy has forgotten what has happened to him, more that he has simply tried to follow the familiar family pattern of trying to look past the bad. "Get on with it," runs the mantra of the stoic, and this is exactly what this family tries to do. But the real-life consequence of "getting on with it" is often a tremendous, eventually debilitating backup of rage and unexpressed sorrow. Hoffman's narrative inevitably builds up subterranean pressure—the pressure of all that undischarged emotion demanding release. As readers, we make a basic psychological assumption: if the emotion does not get released, it may destroy the individual. We should keep in mind, however, that while our reading experience is powerfully affective, it is based on deliberate craft decisions made by the author. In literature as in life, to *not tell* is a strategic manipulation.

Here is the dynamic of *Half the House.* After the closely sequential chapters depicting boyhood traumas come the chronological gaps. We jump from 1964 to 1970, from 1975 to 1984. What happens during these intervals—the all-important developments of young manhood—is kept offstage; we can only make surmises based on the few clues that the author offers us.

Naturally we try to piece together what we can—we are expected to. The chapter headed "1984" is an instance. Here, Hoffman, a man in his mid-thirties, has come home to be with his dying mother (this is the second 1984 chapter, for the memoir also began with this date). After the death, he and his father are together awaiting the arrival of the men from the funeral home. Hoffman's father asks his son to disconnect the oxygen hose. He writes:

> After I had done what he asked, I went into the kitchen and poured myself a tumbler of whiskey.
> "Dickie? Go easy with that, will you?" Aunt Kitty said.
> "What? What are you talking about?"
> "Never mind. Just go easy, that's all."

Hoffman gives us no drawn-out account of his drinking, nothing more than a snapshot or two, but we have our own surmises. We are not surprised when he later tells his father that he fell into alcoholism, that he has had to seek treatment, counseling, and that he still fights to stay sober. The gaps, the unreported years, become an amplifying space. We project into them, imagining a drinking problem commensurate with the undigested trauma that we have witnessed.

As Hoffman keeps a lid on the inevitably sensational story of his painful collapse into alcoholism, so he also keeps to himself the story of his recovery. Were there long years of therapy, ordeals of self-reckoning? The author doesn't tell us. It would be a very different memoir if he did: the focus would be shifted in significant ways onto the psychological consequences, inevitably diluting the presented impact of the traumatic events themselves.

Hoffman concludes *Half the House* as he began, with straightforwardly narrated scenes, and our job is to infer the emotional work he has done. The last section, in structure as well as content, helps us do the work. After the rapid leapfrogging of the earlier chapters, the last five, all dated 1990, tell of two separate visits home. In the first, Hoffman returns alone. He is there for the long-deferred reckoning with his father. Man to man. Fending off an almost intolerable anxiety, he quite literally unpacks his baggage, removing talismanic objects that will help him say what he needs to say:

> I took out a picture of myself at eight and placed it on the coffee table between us. I didn't know how to begin. I reached in the bag again and took out three bronze medallions, one for each year I'd been sober in Alcoholics Anonymous. I reached across the table and held them out to him; they clinked as he turned them over, examining them.
>
> "Do you know what those are?" I asked him.
> "No. Well. I guess I have some idea."

"Those are the medals I won in the war, Dad."

"What war?"

Hoffman finds it wrenching to tell his father the whole story, but his father's initial reflex of downplaying the scale of injury gives him the anger he needs in order to launch forward. Their afternoon is one of revelations and accusations. Not only does Hoffman tell the long-held secret about his coach, but he also makes a devastating link between that abuse and the fact that his father beat him when he was a boy. He introduces this by removing his belt and setting it on the table. The scene offers its father/son dislosures even as it maps the family's familiar psychological pattern:

I shook the belt at him. "You terrorized us," I said. "There's no other word for it. You used to come home from work, from the fuckin' brewery, drunk, I guess, and beat the shit out of me and Bob. I remember screaming and running to get away from you, the two of us on our hands and knees while you swung your belt at us. So don't give me any of this shit about 'spankings.' I was scared to death of you."

"How can that be? I remember playing catch with you in the yard when I came home from work. Of course Bob was too sick. But you and I. When I coached the American Legion team, you went along

to every game. You were the batboy! How come you
don't remember that?"

"Who says I don't remember that?"

"Well you talk as if . . . never mind."

"No, go ahead, say it. There were good times too.
But I'm not talking about good times versus bad times,
Dad. I'm talking about assault and battery on a child."

By the end of Hoffman's stay his father is badly shaken,
but after they make a visit to the family graves a first reconciliation has taken place. Hoffman's father admits to
his guilt, his culpability, and Hoffman, for his part, finally
takes the step of trying to understand what forces and
circumstances have made the man who he was. He pictures what it must have been like for him to come home
from the war where he had served as a paratrooper:

> I imagined my father, schooled in fierceness, home
> from the war, marching under ticker tape and a bliz-
> zard of confetti, as I'd seen it on television over and
> over when I was a boy. I thought of him marching
> away from the slaughter with the others, in forma-
> tion, empty rifles on their shoulders, just the way
> they'd hoped it would be, but hollow and hungover
> and mistaking, like all survivors, relief for pleasure,
> the absence of horror for peace, conventionality for

safety. His dreams were gone, his memories buried. He raised his glass to the future. He married my mother. He went to work in the brewery.

Ashes. Amnesia. Anesthesia.

And rage.

After this difficult visit, Hoffman agrees to return for Thanksgiving. This time he comes with his own son and daughter—his wife elects to stay home—and through the evocation of the crowd of extended family, Hoffman makes very clear the complex encounter of his old life and his new one. There are no easy wrap-ups, no comforting bromides. But in the generational panorama we suddenly discern that a hard, brave victory has been achieved. The family saga has come full circle. Hoffman, sober, a father, has not only lived to tell the tale. He has worked to understand and fashion it into art.

The memoir ends with Hoffman out on the old playground—the very spot where he used to play ball—with his children. They are playing tag, and all of a sudden, without warning, he is laughing and crying, releasing an enormous weight of grief. That his children think he is just laughing kicks up the tension between perspectives, and at the same time releases the powerful emotions we always find when innocence is backgrounded by the unrecognized sorrows of hard experience.

"Boy, Dad, you must have thought of something pretty funny!" Robert says. He looks at me, puzzled. I can't stop. If I could, if I could stop the laughter, I would tell him this is not hilarity, but joy. Veronica yells, "Watch me again!" as she throws herself in the pile of leaves, believing she has made me laugh so hard. I go on laughing, crying, until I am finished.

"Come on," I say, standing and wiping my eyes. "It's time to go home."

If some trauma is experienced as a harsh blow struck from outside—Mary Karr looking up to see her mother coming toward her with a raised butcher knife, Richard Hoffman suffering harsh, confusing sexual initiation at the hands of his football coach—there are also horrors that are meted out gradually, that don't have obvious outside origins. Lucy Grealy was six years old when she collided with a classmate's head on the school playground. The subsequent pain persisted, and led, by slow stages, to the discovery of a cancer that would require the removal of a big part of her jaw and put her on a path of treatment and repeated reconstructive surgery that would make much of the rest of her life an agonizing struggle for normalcy and happiness. Her memoir, *Autobiography of a Face,* records with great feeling and psychological honesty the sequence of events and her efforts to comprehend what was happening to her. At the same time, it locates in her travails an underlying drama of self-recognition, one that culminates in a convincing, if possibly provisional, gesture of self-acceptance.

While the main chapters of the memoir follow the essential chronology of events, Grealy also incorporates the double perspective from the outset, both in the setup of her Prologue and in her consistent use of interpolated hindsight reflections.

The Prologue is both scenic and expository, offering us a certain background context and at the same time enlisting us straightaway in her painful outsider's point of view. The author takes a few pages to fill us in on her situation. At first introduction she is a fourteen-year-old girl working with a friend bringing ponies to a child's birthday party. She re-creates a sense of festivity, the growing excitement as the ponies are unloaded from the trailer, only then telling us the rest: "My pleasure at the sight of the children didn't last long, however. I knew what was coming. As soon as they got over the thrill of being near the ponies, they'd notice me. Half my jaw was missing, which gave my face a strange triangular shape, accentuated by the fact that I was unable to keep my mouth completely closed."

Having given us the harsh truth straight on, Grealy pulls back again, though from this point on we never lose our awareness of her tragic circumstance. The knowledge remains with us as Grealy backtracks to explain how she got the job, and then as she offers an explanatory account of her own family situation, underscoring the difference between her parents—displaced from their native Ireland, at odds with their situation—and the emphatically normal-seeming mothers and fathers she meets at these privileged events.

Grealy brings the scene to its culmination by focusing on the inevitable photo moment. She has set up her opening dexterously, with apparent simplicity bringing together festivity and private dread, normalcy and exceptionality, and, in a powerful modulation, past, present, and future tenses. The two paragraphs deserve to be quoted in full:

> With the same numbed yet cavalier stance, I waited for a father to click the shutter. At least these were photographs I'd never have to see, though to this day I fantasize about meeting someone who eventually shows me their photo album and there, inexplicably, in the middle of a page, is me holding a pony. I have seen one pony party photo of me. In it I'm holding on to a small dark bay pony whose name I don't remember. I look frail and thin and certainly peculiar, but I don't look anywhere near as repulsive as I then believed I did. There's a gaggle of children around me, waiting for their turn on the pony. My stomach was always in knots then, surrounded by so many

children, but I can tell by my expression that I'm convincing myself I don't care as I point to the back of
the line. The children look older than most of the kids
at the backyard parties: some of them are even older
than nine, the age I was when I got sick. I'm probably
thinking about this, too, as I order them into line.

I can still hear the rubbery, metallic thud of
hooves on the trailer's ramp as we loaded the ponies
back into the hot and smelly box for the ride back to
Diamond D. Fifteen years later, when I see that photo,
I am filled with questions I rarely allow myself, such
as, how do we go about turning into the people we
are meant to be? What relation do the human beings
in that picture have to the people they are now? How
is it that all of us were caught together in that brief
moment of time, me standing there pretending I
wasn't hurt by a single thing in this world while they
lined up for their turn on the pony, some of them ex-
cited and some of them scared, but all of them neatly,
at my insistence, one in front of the other, like all the
days ahead.

Examining this passage closely, we see the intricate
blending of perspectives. Grealy deploys her point of
view like a skilled cinematographer, shifting unobtru-
sively from fantasy, to straight description, to hindsight
interpretation, to pure sensory memory, to reflective

questioning, thus giving her reader an advance indication of the complexity that lies in store. The last phrase of the passage is perfectly placed to set up what will follow.

With the first chapter, "Luck," Grealy launches what will be an essentially chronological account of her ever-worsening situation, beginning with the schoolyard accident and the discovery of the growth in her jaw, continuing by excruciating stages the narration of her operation, treatments, and the resulting disfigurement—the "autobiography of a face." But as she will eventually make explicit, the story of her face *is* the story of her own formation; it is the cause of her torments and source of her hard recognitions, and only through her long struggle to master what her body has inflicted does she achieve her identity.

Grealy makes use throughout of an artful fusion of time perspectives, on the one hand giving her account without excessive hindsight revelation, ensuring that at every turn we share her hope that treatments and reconstructive surgeries will give her back the face she had. Indeed, so powerful is her need to believe that we suspend all disbelief to assume it ourselves, along with the racking suspense that comes with anticipated outcomes. We are caught up in the ancient Sophoclean tension: knowing full well that Oedipus will kill his father and marry his mother, we nonetheless follow along in fear and trembling, willing what is not to be.

THE ART OF TIME IN MEMOIR   171

But even as she guides us forward, keeping the central narration in the point of view of the young girl, Grealy reminds us of the hindsight perspective as well, either through direct reference, or else through the implicit power of her voice. This is not a naïve narrator. Her suffering has made her a philosopher, a student of fate, chance, and the complex us/them psychology of the outsider.

We encounter this secondary vantage directly for the first time in the opening chapter, when Grealy sets up her account of the discovery of the malignancy:

> When a film's heroine innocently coughs, you know that two scenes later, at most, she'll be in an oxygen tent; when a man bumps into a woman at the train station, you know that man will become the woman's lover and/or murderer. In everyday life, where we cough often and are always bumping into people, our daily actions rarely reverberate so lucidly. Once we love or hate someone, we can think back and remember that first casual encounter. But what of all the chance meetings that nothing ever comes of? While our bodies move ever forward on the time line, our minds continuously trace backward, seeking shape and meaning as deftly as any arrow seeking its mark.

The quote can stand as representative. Throughout the memoir Grealy makes use of the interwoven reflection, almost as if she were adapting the old dramatic convention of the soliloquy.

Grealy's title—*Autobiography of a Face*—proves to be the guiding trope of the book, inviting us to take the part for the whole and to consider her life profoundly determined by the drama of appearances. The face claims our main attention throughout. From the first chapter on we have, following Grealy's lead, invested ourselves in the possibility of successful treatment and reconstruction, and we read *as if.* As if the long narration of pain is a prelude to redemption; as if we will look back in the end and see it all as a trial, a rite of passage; as if Grealy's "real" face is the retrieved, repaired face. She believes this, and we endorse her belief.

For this reason, some of the most disturbing scenes in the book are the scenes of objective self-confrontation—mirror scenes. There are several, and each is presented to crushing effect, reminding us how, like Grealy, we have allowed ourselves to cling to the myth of progress.

One day, for instance, fairly late in the chronology, when Grealy has already gone through the ordeal of reconstruction, she accompanies her mother shopping:

> Pulling the new shirt on over my head, I caught a
> glimpse of my reflection in a mirror that was itself
> being reflected in a mirror opposite, reversing my
> face as I usually saw it. I stood there motionless, the

shirt only halfway on, my skin extra pale from the lighting, and saw how asymmetrical my face was. How had that happened? Walking up to the mirror, reaching up to touch the right side, where the graft had been put in only a year before, I saw clearly that most of it had disappeared, melted away into nothing. I felt distraught at the sight and even more distraught that it had taken so long to notice. My eyes had been secretly working against me, making up for the asymmetry as it gradually reappeared. This reversed image of myself was the true image, the way other people saw me.

I felt like such a fool. I'd been walking around with a secret notion of promised beauty, and here was the reality.

Truths like the one Grealy must face here are brutal. No single recognition can quite undo the long practice of denial. But later in the memoir, as she grows older, travels, begins living on her own, suffers the failure of further reconstructive initiatives, she is slowly brought closer to recognition. Her culminating insight comes one evening when she is sitting with a man in a café. She has, as she reports, been staying away from mirrors. But now, she writes, "I suddenly wondered what I looked like to him. What was he actually *seeing* in me? . . . I had no ready answer. I had not looked in a mirror for so long that I had no idea what I objectively looked like." That adverb "objectively" draws the line, reminding us by no means for the first time of the powerful split between outer appearance and inner imagining. So long as Grealy has dreamed the unattainable face, she has had to deem the external an aberration—she has had to live with a terrible sense of self-separation. The mirror symbolizes this, and the reflection she forces herself to study ratifies it. But now, for whatever reason, she is ready to try to heal the split. As she puts it: "I experienced a moment of the freedom I'd been practicing for behind my Halloween mask all those years ago. As a child I had expected my liberation to come from getting a new face to put on, but now I saw it came from shedding something, shedding my image." Being witness in this way to the self's encounter with its assumptions and illusions, the private reckoning given literary form, is one of the deep rewards of reading memoir. We are drawn up close to the life of another and, if the moment is presented with artistic skill, we invariably find ways to connect its larger implications to our own experience.

Grealy finally lets go of the illusion, the denial, and comes to grips with the tyranny of appearances that has made her ventures into the world so difficult. She understands: "Society is no help. It tells us again and again that we can most be ourselves by acting and looking like someone else, only to leave our original faces behind to turn into ghosts that will inevitably resent and haunt us."

And then, perhaps more believable for being tentative, lowercase, she tells us how she dares the next small but all-important step:

> As I sat there in the café, it suddenly occurred to me that it is no mistake when sometimes in films the dead know they are dead only after being offered that most irrefutable proof: they can no longer see themselves in the mirror.
>
> Feeling the warmth of the cup against my palm, I felt this small observation as a great revelation. I wanted to tell the man I was with about it, but he was involved in his own thoughts and I did not want to interrupt him, so instead I looked with curiosity at the window behind him, its night-silvered glass reflecting the entire café, to see if I could, now, recognize myself.

I should say here that though I did not know Lucy Grealy well, she was for some years my colleague at the Bennington Writing Seminars, and on two occasions I had the privilege of teaching a nonfiction workshop with her. Lucy was the "truth-serum" teacher, more willing than most to offer the challenging, unsweetened response, to announce when a passage in a workshop essay struck her as boring, or false, or to weed it for faulty syntax. Students were often nervous about her judgments, and I sometimes chafed at being the "good cop" at the other end of the table. But when we talked writer-talk by ourselves, I understood how much she suffered to get her sentences right, and how remorselessly she turned that scouring eye on her own expression. Lucy performed her own version of "Physician, heal thyself" with a rigor that still heartens me some years after her unhappy death.

Dealing with the deepest kinds of psychological injuries, trauma-based memoirs are by definition disturbing. But of the four works I chose to discuss, Kathryn Harrison's *The Kiss* was, for me, the most unsettling. Apart from the author's palpable anguish—over the relationship that all but tore her life apart—there is the matter of the taboo. We read of a young woman's sexual relationship—her "affair"—with her biological father. Never mind that he left his family shortly after Harrison's birth, the sense of primal violation is electric. Harrison's own collusion, her long-term prostration before the power of the father's need, makes the confession hard to read, the twisted fascination of the subject notwithstanding. We do not respond calmly to self-abasement and psychological self-mortification. At the same time, we cannot dispute the author's need to give release to the experience, or her courage about doing so publicly.

The Kiss is a short book. For all the weight of implication of its various revelations, it moves with a breathless momentum. Composed of short episodes rendered almost entirely in the present tense, making shrewd use of suspense, the memoir reaches us not through the customary strategy of sustained immersion but instead by way of a series of hard blows to the plexus. We absorb many of its suggestions only after the fact.

Much of the grave poignancy of the work comes from the fact that it tells two powerful—and psychologically fused—stories, surprising us in the end with what feels at first like a displacement of focus, but has to be seen eventually as a push to a deeper emotional truth. What I mean is that while the memoir is, at first blush (pun intended), about Harrison's erotic compulsion toward her long-lost father, it is ultimately the story of her difficult psychological reconciliation with her mother.

"We meet at airports. We meet in cities where we've never been before. We meet where no one will recognize us." Mystery, provocation, the time-honored Aristotelian in medias res opening. And to make sure we appreciate the stakes, Harrison waits only a few sentences before sinking the hook: "Against such backdrops, my father takes my face in his hands. He tips it up and kisses my closed eyes, my throat." Harrison knows very well that she is tapping the power of the taboo, and throughout this short work she stages scenes for dramatic effect, delaying whatever will be the next shocking revelation until the last possible moment, thus upping its frisson power.

After she has captured our attention, Harrison steps back to fill in, much as Karr did after her opening tableau. We move to the past, in short present-tense takes, getting glimpses of Harrison's childhood, the meeting of her parents, their separation, everything we need in order to understand the possibility, if not plausibility, of what will follow.

Once the backdrop has been given, however, Harrison chooses to pay out the narrative slowly, dropping suggestive hints, but then pulling back, setting up the story of the first adult encounter between father and daughter. "It begins when I'm twenty," she writes. "It begins with a visit." Capitalizing on the natural tension that builds on any approach to a foreordained event, Harrison deliberately takes many pages getting us to the explosive scene of the first transgression, the one from which all else follows.

Anyone working with narrative—memoiristic, fictional, or documentary—would do well to study this tactic and its underlying principle: <u>where sufficient suspense has been created, interruption and digression</u>

(controlled, of course) can heighten rather than diminish the effect. Readers will wait eagerly for resolution, for the other shoe to drop, but they must not have forgotten the sound of the first shoe hitting the floor.

In fact, the kiss, the breakthrough violation, is not unforeseen (the opening passage tells us what we need to know); nor is it, if we heed the psychology as Harrison presents it, altogether unwelcome. The father's lifelong absence has created a vacuum in the young woman that changes, and in a way explains, everything that happens.

The original shocking contact is anticipated and created by the gaze, by the recognition Harrison experiences at the father's visit (ostensibly to see her mother, his ex-wife) when the three are together in the mother's house:

> I don't know it yet, not consciously, but I feel it: my father, holding himself so still and staring at me, has somehow begun to *see* me into being. His look gives me to myself, his gaze reflects the life my mother's willfully shut eyes denied. Looking at him looking at me, I cannot help but fall painfully, precipitously in love. And my loving him is inseparable from a piercing sense of loss. Whenever I am alone—in my bedroom, the bathroom—I find myself crying, sometimes even sinking to my knees. How am I to endure this new despair? How can it be that I am twenty years old, that I've had to grow up without a father, only to

meet him now when it's too late, when childhood is over, lost?

This is the effective prelude to the moment that only comes when Harrison has taken her father back to the airport, and they are saying good-bye:

> A voice over the public-address system announces the final boarding call for my father's flight. As I pull away, feeling the resistance of his hand behind my head, how tightly he holds me to him, the kiss changes. It is no longer a chaste, closed-lip kiss.
> My father pushes his tongue deep into my mouth: wet, insistent, exploring, then withdrawn.

Here we confront it straight on, the incest taboo, and our reaction (my reaction, anyway) reveals its on-going power. I am disturbed, drawn in, thrown into a confusion about intimacies and boundaries, and very much aware that transgression tends to exact its penalties. Harrison reaches deep into the reader's privacy, stirring things up; she also creates—implicitly—a narrative expectation. Something very serious will have to come of this.

The middle part of the memoir is, from a narrative point of view, orchestrated around the flashpoint scenes, each one marking another step deeper into the incestuous, each rendering Harrison more abject in her collusion, more powerless. After the kiss come the letters and phone calls, the complete saturation of her formerly independent life by the insistent presence of the father. The daughter all but melts into the strange heat of the father's need, giving up on her college studies, her boyfriend, eventually just dropping out. They take trips together, and while at first she resists his bids for complete sexual intimacy, he eventually breaks her down. When Harrison finds she cannot make a writing life for herself in New York City, her father invites her to live with him and her stepmother and their daughter, and there, under his own family roof, he fulfills his obsession.

Only now, by degrees, does Harrison begin to discover a detachment about the relationship, and with it a slowly growing reluctance. What she is actually realizing, at a deep unconscious level, is how much the whole terrible cycle has to do with her mother—and how this is true both for her father and herself.

The realization has been prepared in an earlier scene, when, after another of the father's "visits," Harrison comes back from the airport to find her mother pacing in the living room. "'There's something wrong with all of this,' she says. 'I feel it.'" She knows nothing, but her instincts are alert to the energy passing between her daughter and her ex-husband. And a moment later she announces: "'You know . . . this isn't about *you*. It's about *me*.'" Harrison pauses here to insert the hindsight perspective: "Years after my mother's death, I'll know that she was right." Then, reading letters her father once wrote to her mother, she will see how on every page they create what will be the template for his assertions and protestations to her. There should be a name for this maneuver, a degree-of-difficulty calculation like the one used for skating and gymnastics. Harrison moves from the narrative present, to a flash-forward confirmation ("Years after . . ."), and then invokes the past of the letters, only applying the insights gained through further hindsight refraction. The amazing thing is that as readers we follow, integrating, adjusting, ultimately deepening our understanding.

The last third of *The Kiss* enacts a complicated turn from father to mother, effecting the most painful liberation from what has become a soul-strangling mutual tyranny. First there is the slow realization of the damage. "My father's possessing me seems to be just that," she writes. "Each time, he takes a little more of my life; each time, there is less of me left."

But realization and actual change of behavior are two different things. The will to change does not come until she finds out that her mother is dying of cancer. Only then, with the feeling of a tidal shift, does Harrison grasp the full depth of her need for her mother's love. She can finally understand how it has all along been the woman's core unavailability that has twisted her fate and her father's into a knot. Now as she is dying, her emotions find release and compel her to break the deadlock.

Interestingly, the first major turn is caused by proxy, as it were—by the death of her grandfather. Harrison feels a powerful compulsion to go to the morgue to view the body. It is almost as if she needs the physical proof of finality to make some essential connection for herself:

> Though I've courted and teased death, played irresponsibly with my life, I never believed in my own mortality until I sat beside my grandfather's cold body, touched and smelled and embraced it. All along, it was my unbelief that made recklessness possible. The hour I spent with my grandfather, kneeling by the long drawer, changes my life. The kiss I place on his unyielding cheek begins to wake me, just as my father's at the airport put me to sleep. I am transformed from a person who assumed she had time to squander to one who now knows that no matter how many years her fate holds, there will not be enough.

Harrison is at last ready. Two pages later she reports to her grandmother that she is preparing to apply to graduate schools.

The next scene, literal and symbolic at once, is the clincher. In a rash move that recalls the ascetic mortifications of saints, Harrison cuts off her long hair before going to visit her mother at the hospital. With typical cunning of deflation, her mother scarcely reacts, saying only, "'It's about time,'" and then, moments later, "'There you are. All anyone's seen for years was hair.'" Harrison offers the translation, making clear what she knows to be the unspoken message, making use of an almost didactic tone of voice:

> Long hair is an obvious symbol of sexuality, and for me it was the safeguard of my femaleness when I'd given up my breasts and my period. By cutting my hair off, I tell my mother that my sexual life is severed as well. Discarding it, I promise her that she can die knowing the affair between her daughter and her husband is finished.

With this sacrifice the mother/daughter struggle is ended, and when, soon after, Harrison's mother dies, the response, discharging years of blocked-off emotion, is powerfully redemptive:

> I touch her chest, her arms, her neck; I kiss her forehead and her fingertips; I lay my warm cheek against her cold one; and, as I do, something drops away from me: that slick, invisible, impenetrable wall. Whatever it was that separated me from my life, from the life I had before I met my father—the remains of what

was built in an instant by his long-ago kiss—comes suddenly down. And as it does I gasp, I squeeze my mother's fingers. *Oh God, I'm sorry, I'm sorry,* I say. *My God, oh God,* it's *over.*

Harrison has used elements of dramatic tragedy throughout, most obviously the incest theme, which points straight back to Sophocles. Fittingly, then, she finds ways—as here—to bring emotional release, catharsis, into her presentation. What she has portrayed as her terrible transgressions are in the later pages of the book balanced by scenes of confrontation, confession, and reconciliation.

Breaking with her father is all at once easy and essentially uncontested. The dissipation of tensions has changed everything at a stroke. She offers him the possibility of a more normal father/daughter relationship—visits, communications—but he will not hear of it. "'Don't you know me yet?'" he asks. "'Don't you know my answer?'" And indeed: "What else have the last years taught me if not that my father will take nothing less than all of me?"

The drama is done with, the sorrow expressed Harrison is at last free to move into her own life, as free as a person so compelled and susceptible is likely to be. We know from flash-forward passages in the book that she has gone on to marry and have children of her own.

She and her husband have an understanding: "In our marriage we've made a place for my father and what happened between me and him. It's a locked place, the psychic equivalent of a high cupboard, nearly out of reach."

In the very last section, as a coda, Harrison reports on a vivid dream she had many years after her mother's death. Her mother has come to find Harrison in the kitchen. Standing there, she looks beautiful, exquisitely tailored, but she shrugs off her daughter's compliments. We wait. There is no reproach, no confrontation. Mother and daughter are somehow together in an understanding beyond all conflict. Harrison uses the moment to conclude the book:

> Nothing happens then, and yet everything transpires. My mother and I look closely at each other. We look into each other's eyes more deeply than we ever did in life, and for much longer. Our eyes don't move or blink, they are no more than a few inches apart. As we look, all that we have ever felt but have never said is manifest. Her youth and selfishness and misery, my youth and selfishness and misery. Our loneliness. The ways we betrayed each other.
>
> In this dream, I feel that at last she knows me, and I her. I feel us stop hoping for a different daughter and a different mother.

The push to reconciliation is powerful in all of us. In the memoirist it often proves to be both the instigating impulse and the sustaining force. We can take a confirming look back, at Karr and her mother driving home together after too many margaritas, or at Grealy searching out her reflection in the café window, or Wolff hugging his sons, or Gornick sitting with her now aged mother . . . The writing is in every case propelled by the need to find closure in the self, to make pattern from contingency, and to enact the drama of claiming a self from the chaos of possibility. For this reason, inescapably, memoir requires that a balance be struck between then and now, event and understanding. The manipulation of perspectives is but the means for achieving this. It reflects the restless search for sense that is universal, but which achieves its most realized expression in the artistic memoir.

While these recountings of trauma may abound in surprising or suspenseful scenes, the fact that the work exists argues that the writer attained some eventual reconciliation or mastery. The ultimate outcome, in other words, is not at issue. The vital tension, however, is not thereby stripped away so much as it is redirected. Since we read within a horizon of reassurance, we engage more deeply in the psychological process itself, and this carries its own escalating excitements.

Knowing that the princess is finally rescued by her prince doesn't do away with our fear and trembling—we all grant this—and in the same way, knowing that someone survived a hellish life situation to write about it does not reduce either our empathy or our eventual relief.

Coda

The fact that so many memoirs make use of some logic of circularity, reminding the reader at the end of their point of origin, encourages me to make a similar circuit-completing gesture. Maybe it's the writer-turned-teacher announcing himself, wanting to be sure that he has hammered his message home. But where the teacher can raise the question directly—"Did you all understand that?"—or at least scan the room for the telltale signs of incomprehension, the writer can only bluntly reassert.

I observed at the outset that the memoir has suffered from a certain backlash in recent years, that there exists a public perception—though by no means universal—that the genre is glorified navel-gazing, more than a little narcissistic, an outgrowth of our talk-show fixation on dysfunction and the ethos of self-help. Indeed, I've even heard people venture that the writing of memoirs is more a therapeutic than an artistically expressive occupation, and that the results are best put away in the desk drawer rather than shopped in the marketplace.

I could not disagree more. If our sultans of commerce have looked to turn a profit from works of sensational confession—and God knows there is no shortage of these, both straight-faced and opportunistic—they have done the same with every other genre since publishing began. My main hope in writing this reflective survey has been to argue for the complexity and sophistication of the literary memoir and at the same time to insist that there is a necessary wisdom in the best of these works that cannot be discovered in the other genre, not in the same way.

The point—the glory—of memoir is that it anchors its authority in the actual life; it is a modeling of the process of creative self-inquiry as it is applied to the stuff of lived experience. *This really happened* is the baseline contention of the memoir, and the fascination of the work—apart from the interest we have in what is told—is in tracking the artistic transformation of the actual via the alchemy of psychological insight, pattern recognition, and lyrical evocation into a contained saga. Every memoir is a more or less successful working out of the old Socratic injunction: "Know thyself." There is nothing here for readers to question or contest. The pressure on the individual to find meaning—an integrated narrative of personal experience—is as intense as it has ever been, and the need for exemplary works, for vicarious enactments, is, if anything, growing.

Memoir is a narrative art, but through its careful manipulation of vantage point it simulates the subjective sense of experience apprehended through memory and the corrective actions of hindsight. In other words it gives artistic form to what is the main business of our ongoing inner life. Memoir returns to the past, investigating causes in the light of their known effects, conjuring the unresolved mysteries of fate versus chance, free will versus determinism. To read the life of another person put before us in this way is inevitably to repossess something of ourselves. The writer's *then* and *now* stir to life our own sense of past and present. So long as we believe ourselves to be living in the direction of meaning, memoir will never not be coming into its own, fresh and startling.

Books Cited

Aciman, André: *The Proust Project*
Ackerley, J. R.: *My Dog Tulip*
Adams, Henry: *The Education of Henry Adams*
Augustine, Saint: *Confessions*
Auster, Paul: *The Invention of Solitude*
Baker, Russell: *Growing Up*
Beard, Jo Ann: *The Boys of My Youth*
Bergson, Henri: *Matter and Memory*
Blaise, Clark: *I Had a Father*
Canetti, Elias: *The Tongue Set Free*
Catullus: *Complete Poems*
Cheever, Susan: *Home Before Dark*
Conroy, Frank: *Stop-Time*
Dillard, Annie: *An American Childhood*
García Márquez, Gabriel: *Living to Tell the Tale*
Gornick, Vivian: *Fierce Attachments*
Gosse, Edmund: *Fathers and Sons*
Grealy, Lucy: *Autobiography of a Face*
Harrison, Kathryn: *The Kiss*
Hoffman, Eva: *Lost in Translation*
Hoffman, Richard: *Half the House*
Howard, Maureen: *Facts of Life*
Karr, Mary: *The Liars' Club*
Kincaid, Jamaica: *Annie John*
Larkin, Philip: *Collected Poems*

Lowell, Robert: *Collected Poems*
Mallarmé, Stéphane: *Complete Poems*
Mandelstam, Nadezhda: *Hope Against Hope* and
    Hope Abandoned
McCourt, Frank: *Angela's Ashes*
Merwin, W. S.: *Unframed Originals*
Mill, John Stuart: *Autobiography*
Miller, Sue: *The Story of My Father*
Moody, Rick: *The Black Veil*
Morrison, Blake: *And When Did You Last See Your Father?*
Nabokov, Vladimir: *Speak, Memory*
Ondaatje, Michael: *Running in the Family*
Pound, Ezra: *Cantos*
Proust, Marcel: *Remembrance of Things Past*
Sterne, Laurence: *Tristram Shandy*
West, Paul: *My Mother's Music*
Wolff, Geoffrey: *The Duke of Deception*
Wolff, Tobias: *This Boy's Life*
Woolf, Virginia: *Moments of Being*
Yourcenar, Marguerite: *Memoirs of Hadrian*

SVEN BIRKERTS is the author of eight books, including *Reading Life: Books for the Ages, The Gutenberg Elegies: The Fate of Reading in an Electronic Age, Readings*, and *My Sky Blue Trades: Growing Up Counter in a Contrary Time*. He has received a fellowship from the Guggenheim Foundation, the Citation for Excellence in Reviewing from the National Book Critics Circle, and the Spielvogel-Diamonstein Award from PEN. Birkerts has reviewed regularly for the *New York Times Book Review*, the *New Republic, Esquire*, the *Washington Post*, the *Atlantic, Mirabella, Parnassus*, the *Yale Review*, and other publications. He is a member of the core faculty of the Bennington Writing Seminars and has taught at Emerson College, Amherst College, and Mt. Holyoke College. Birkerts is currently the editor of *AGNI* and the Briggs-Copeland lecturer at Harvard University. He lives in Arlington, Massachusetts, with his wife and two children.

The text of *The Art of Time in Memoir: Then, Again* is set in Warnock Pro, a typeface designed by Robert Slimbach for Adobe Systems in 2000. Book design by Wendy Holdman. Composition by Prism Publishing Center. Manufactured by Versa Press on acid-free paper.